Who Says You Can't Be Happy?

(A Handbook for Happiness)

By Dr. Karen Parsonson

WHO SAYS YOU CAN'T BE HAPPY?

(Handbook for Happiness)

Acknowledgements

There have been numerous people in my life who have been an inspiration for this book and I'll start chronologically. To my dearest grandparents, both the Gevogas and Parsonsons, who believed in me from when I first opened my eyes...especially to my Grampa Gevoga, who filled me with the wonder of the world around me and my own place in it. To my parents: my Mom who is gone now but still in my heart and believed in me through everything and my Dad who is sadly no longer with us, who cheered me on and provided me with his wisdom and never-ending love. To my god-parents, Aunty Lou and Uncle Jack who were always there for me, always loving and unconditionally supportive. To my daughter Rebecca, wise beyond her years, beautiful, talented in so many ways and who has taught me so much. To my son Josh, whose sensitivity, loving-kindness and gentleness have helped me grow as a person. To my life-partner, soul-mate, husband and best-friend Adison, who has encouraged me, loved me unconditionally and believed in me throughout our time together. There are many others: my "frister" Tammy and wonderful friend Catherine among them who made me feel like what I had to say was worth saying.

Preface:

I recently sat at a 3-day conference, diligently taking notes, as I always do. My mind began to wander, thinking to myself: I know that, I do that, but this way works better...I began to realize how much more I had learned from the years of working with the people who trusted me enough to share their lives, their sadness and their joys for so many years.

Having worked as a psychologist for over 25 years with individuals, couples and families, I am struck by the recurring patterns I see in people's lives. Everyone is so different, yet all are searching for the key to their own happiness. Many have been in therapy for years with numerous therapists, some are just beginning. It makes me sad to see how long some have been searching and I thought it was time to cut through the jargon, the "psychobabble", the endless over-analysis. These are some of the kernels of truth I have learned from working with people throughout the years, so much more than any text-books I ever had to read. I hope they can provide some short-cuts to achieving your goals faster.

Contents

Chapter 1

The Premise of Counseling: Why Do it?

It takes a lot of courage to see a therapist or counselor, to open up about your deepest, darkest secrets, memories, feelings and wishes. I am forever amazed and thankful for the trust my patients placed in me to help them deal with their lives from the past, in the present, and for the future. In my mind, they are the strong ones who recognize that things could be a little easier but they just haven't found the way yet. It isn't that they haven't been able to cope with life up to this point. They have survived with varying levels of success, but want to get over past issues that keep getting in the way and burdening them or to figure out ways of dealing with current issues in their lives that trouble them.

When I meet someone for the first time, I make it clear that it's a team effort. What we talk about and do in an hour can rarely change a person's life. It's about what they do with it in between, the "homework" of life in the meantime. The privacy of a therapeutic relationship is comforting, because they know that what we talk about goes nowhere outside of the room, unless they plan on hurting themselves or someone else, in which case our duty is to protect them or anyone else who could be hurt. In that case, a therapist has to call in family or the authorities (depending upon the legal requirements for their jurisdiction).

What is the job of a therapist? My daughter said it best when she was about 7 years old and explained to people that her mommy was a "head doctor and heart doctor". When I asked her what that meant, she said: "You're a head doctor because you help people think things through and you're a heart doctor because you make people feel happy!" I used to explain to her that we didn't make people happy...we helped them make **themselves** happier.

You might ask why I chose this career and that is a good question. I was totally focused on a career in medicine and taking pre-med courses when I decided to take psychology as an option. I was sold on it, having found my passion in life. As I was growing up, my dear mother, who stayed at home to raise my brother and I, was the mother that all of my friends turned to for advice. They'd come over for a pop and while we were talking in the kitchen, my mother would be cleaning up after dinner or preparing it for them to stay over, and they'd share their upsets and worries with her, too. She became the "shrink from the sink", as my friends called her, as I'd be chatting to them on the phone and they'd ask Mom what she thought. It made her so happy to be able to help and they'd loved her compassion and wisdom. She was always able to think from her head and her heart, as well. It was inevitable, given how much I am told I am like my mother, that my joy would be found in being a mother and in helping others feel better.

Working on yourself is the hardest job a person can do, because we are so used to living inside ourselves that we have no other perspective. That's what a therapist is there to help with. Friends and family love you and most often accept you. They are our mirrors from the outside world, sometimes giving critical feedback, but not telling you how to get there. We're here to help you take the steps to achieving whatever goals you set out for yourself, one step at a time.

Counseling is a relationship between two people with a common goal: to help the person achieve what they want to in life, in love, in relationships, in their job, in anything. But it's a learning experience for both. Each person's life is a puzzle to me that I try and understand through them how to put the pieces together. As I ask questions and try to fit everything together, so does the other person see the flow of what has happened in his or her life. It is a clarifying experience, to understand what experiences lead to new ones and why. It's about understanding the patterns of what we do, how we interact, what triggers us to react, how we think and why.

So why go to see someone else when we can get advice from friends or family? After all, many have known us our whole lives. And that's the issue...they're emotionally involved, which colors their perceptions. A therapist can give a fresh perspective because our only motivation is to try and understand, to help motivate a person to grow. No one can make anyone change, they have to want to grow. Life is about growth, from birth to death. My very wise mother-in-law, who passed away some years ago and was herself a social worker of many years, said it best when she explained that she would continue growing until she died. And she did...keep growing. What an inspiration, a powerhouse who learned to use a computer in her eighties better than I and took every experience as a learning one. Even after her first stroke that nearly killed her, she relearned to walk and talk. Even with her walker and oxygen tank, she still experienced every bit of life with joy, relishing each new experience with a passion.

Surviving or merely existing is one thing, but **living** should be with a **passion**. Everyone should have a passion in their life...not just for someone else, but for something they love doing. For some, it may be their work. Not everyone is lucky enough to love their work, but some of us do. For others, it may be a hobby, a sport, an activity that keeps them going. Searching for and finding that passion, whether it's something you do alone or with someone else should be a driving force. I've seen people live for golf or playing pool or tennis or badminton or squash or baseball or hockey or lacrosse or swimming or horse-back riding or skiing or snow-boarding or football or rugby or working-out. Others love to ball-room dance or do aerobics or practice yoga or go to meditation or fly planes or go white-water rafting or hang-gliding. Some love to play an instrument, some love to do crafts, while some love to sew or knit or crochet. For some people, their pets are their passion and they avidly collect them and care for them. For others, their spirituality and religion is their passion, a driving force that gives them some purpose.

Why do people seek therapy? Many have issues with their past relationships that impact on current relationships. Unresolved grief, anger and hurt from the past can certainly affect how we feel and what we do in the present and future. Many have problems with current relationships, the communication, honesty, respect and trust that keep it "real". Some have longstanding anxiety or depression that interferes with their daily lives, success and happiness. Many have forgotten how to be happy, how to do things that make them feel happy, how to think positively, having turned off their feelings to cope with sadness.

Therapy is about understanding ourselves, what we want out of life, what we need, what we dream about, what makes us feel good and how to get there. It's also about understanding others: their intentions, their feelings, their wants and needs. There is so much miscommunication, so many assumptions made, so much misunderstanding within ourselves and between people that it's no wonder life can become confusing. If we can clarify things for ourselves so that we know where we're coming from and where we're going, that's a great beginning.

There are definite patterns in our lives that seem to repeat themselves without us even knowing it. Being able to clearly see the flow of our lives up to this point lets us see what works and what doesn't, what has made us happy and what hasn't, what has made us feel successful and what hasn't. Understanding how our thoughts affect our feelings and our behaviors is crucial, from my perspective. It is described and documented by Frederickson (2001, 2010) as a "positive spiral" or a "negative spiral". If we think positively about ourselves, we feel better about ourselves and are more likely to do good things for ourselves, which then makes us think more positively about ourselves and feel more worthy of doing more positive things for ourselves, and so on (the "positive spiral"). If we think negatively about ourselves, we feel worse about ourselves and are less likely to do good things for ourselves, which then makes us feel more negatively about ourselves and feel less worthy of doing positive things for ourselves, and so on (the "negative spiral").

Let me give a very good personal example. Years ago, when my daughter was little, she would see me coming home from the mall or making special meals or treats for the family. One day, she innocently said to me: "Mummy, you love Joshie and I, don't you? I know because you always make us special things or do specials things with us or buy us things. You love Daddy, too, because you always make him things or buy him special things." Then, she looked me right in the eye and said to me: "You don't love yourself very much, do you, because you don't do special things for yourself or buy anything for yourself?" From the mouths of babes...she had pointed out so clearly to me that if we don't treat ourselves well, in the eyes of others, we don't feel good about ourselves and don't see ourselves as worthy of being treated well by them. If a person doesn't show that they deserve to be treated well, others will respond in kind. In my push to make everyone else feel good, I had forgotten that we can't just feel good because we make others feel good. If we don't take care of ourselves, who else is going to?

Therapy is about emotional nurturance, taking care of oneself emotionally, finding out how you really feel and why. Remember the old joke: "Doctor, doctor, it hurts when I do this." "So stop doing it!"? It's about stopping doing what hurts and discovering what feels good. It is not for the faint-hearted, because it takes hard work to look inside yourself and really see what you need to, to remember what you've forgotten because it hurts too much.

I see our minds as a big filing drawer, each file filled with a different memory. Attached to those memories are feelings about what happened, sometimes good and sometimes bad. For some memories, we process, deal with, accept the feelings and get on with life. For others, we don't - maybe because it's too painful to feel them, but they come out in other ways. Let's say a person has had a terrifying experience and tries to forget it, but the feelings of dread or anxiety or fear persist into new situations. This magnifies the feelings of what may be quite benign situations and the person doesn't know why. It's like "Ghost-busters": the feelings are just hanging out there, waiting to attach themselves to a new situation. Therapy is about opening up those files and releasing the feelings in a safe place, as painful as they may be, so that the file and the drawer can be closed on that chapter of our lives. It's about closing file drawers on the past so that we can get on with experiencing life untainted by past feelings, a fresh start.

Chapter 2

You are Not Your Symptoms

People experience pain, hurt, sadness, fear, anxiety and other negative emotions in so many different ways. Some manifest them physically, in ulcers, migraine headaches, chest pains and other assorted aches or pains. They go to see their doctors and are given tests to assess their hearts, their brain-waves, and their blood for hormone levels, glucose levels and thyroid levels, often to be told there is nothing physically wrong with them. Yet they feel pain or discomfort, physical weakness, an inability to concentrate, among other symptoms. With no apparent reason for feeling this way, some are given pain-killers or anti-depressants or anti-anxiety medication, to help alleviate the symptoms. It doesn't detract from the reasons for feeling that way: we feel for a reason, and masking the symptoms doesn't help with understanding why.

Some people are told they're just "depressed" or "anxious" or "overly sensitive", or "high strung". So how does that help? Trying to figure out why they feel this way, helping them see what has caused it, to change their perceptions, their thoughts, their ways of thinking about it and for the future should be the focus. We can't change what has happened in a person's life, but we can help change how they view it, how they feel about it, stop it from affecting them for the rest of their lives. The object is to stop past experiences from affecting them as much emotionally or physically, to remember them as having happened but not continuing to react to internal or external cues that remind them of how they felt.

We live in a society that likes to categorize or pigeon-hole people...this one is bipolar, that one has generalized anxiety, he's suffering from post-traumatic stress disorder, she has panic attacks...potentially condemning people to a lifetime of the same symptoms. I remember years ago when I was a child reading one of my favorite Archie comic digests about Betty getting hold of a medical dictionary and exhibiting every one of the symptoms she read about, diagnosing herself with some bizarre medical disorder and driving herself up the wall. The school librarian later said that everyone who read it did the same thing. Don't get me wrong, there are genuine diagnoses of psychological/psychiatric disorders, but if you read our diagnostics manual, you'll see some of yourself in everyone.

Understanding where the symptoms come from and dealing with them as our body's or our mind's way of coping with situations is where therapy comes in. The reason our body experiences physical pain is to tell us that something hurts, to protect us from hurting ourselves more, and a medical doctor's job is to find out why in order to treat it. Our mind signals emotional pain or anxiety in order to tell us that it hurts, and to protect us from recurrences. It is a therapist's job to help find out why and treat it. The problem is that there is no physical treatment for a broken heart or emotional bruises. They don't show up on x-rays or MRI's or a physical examination.

If we look at the symptoms of someone who is called "depressed", they include potential sleep problems (can't sleep enough, sleep too much), eating problems (no appetite, too much of an appetite), problems with concentration (not able to focus), lethargy (no stamina from lack of sleep), body aches and pains, among others. They all fit together into a pattern. Whether the person is diagnosed as "clinically depressed" or not, this spectrum of symptoms needs to be addressed individually and as a whole. For some people who experience these symptoms as recurring or totally debilitating, medication in the form of anti-depressants may be necessary to "bump up" their energy to work on getting better.

Similarly, if we examine the symptoms of someone who is anxious, whether they are diagnosed as "generalized anxiety disorder" or "post-traumatic stress disorder" (which has a combination of symptoms from depression and anxiety), there are specific target physical and emotional experiences that interfere with everyday life. These can include chest pains, headaches, stomach complaints, impending feelings of doom, "panic attacks", paralyzing fear and avoidance of situations that produce the anxiety. Just as for depressive symptoms, medication in the form of anti-anxiety or anti-depressants may be necessary to help them cope better. Often, anxiety and depression exist hand-in-hand, as being anxious all the time can limit one's life to the point that it's depressing and feeling depressed all the time can create anxiety from not coping with daily life.

The symptoms of "bipolar disorder" or manic-depression include the depressive symptoms, as well as "manic" jags of behavior and thought. The classic example is of the workaholic who works for 60, 80 or 100 hours straight and then crashes emotionally and physically for several days, only to continue the same pattern. In actual fact, this "mania" may not be expressed in excessive work at all, but in excessive drinking binges or uncontrollable shopping or exercise or sex drive, among others. Whereas everyone has a rhythm of "ups-and-downs", these individuals have huge "peaks and valleys" that make it hard to stabilize and get back up again. Their cycles change over time, as well, in terms of intensity and duration.

Given the boom in diagnosis of childhood and adult attention deficit disorder, everyone knows there are a constellation of symptoms of inattention, impulsivity and hyperactivity. It is often diagnosed for the first time during the early school years and is characterized as the child who is "driven by a motor", or "can't sit still", but this is only for the hyperactive version. In those who don't exhibit the hyperactive, disruptive side, they are impeded by an inability to concentrate or focus. The difference is that only their mind wanders, not their body and they are often not noticed as early as their "hyperactive" counterparts.

Then, there are the "personality disorders": there are so many and include Anti-Social, Avoidant, Borderline, Depressive, Obsessive-Compulsive, Paranoid, Schizoid,...These are simply enduring personality patterns with a constellation of symptoms that are not conducive to successful relationships, success in life and dealing with the world in healthy ways. It is much harder to deal with these symptoms because they are more fixed in a set way of thinking about, reacting to, and interacting with the world.

All symptoms are to varying degrees and people cope with them differently. Some people may have been depressed or anxious for years but they can somehow "push through it" and manage to succeed quite well. They can do the motions that are necessary to survive and even succeed, but they don't feel the success. Sometimes, an experience floors them and brings things crashing down so that they can't cope. Sometimes, they have a physical ailment that is so debilitating that they can't hold back the impact of their emotions (whether they having knowingly suppressed them or unknowingly repressed them) and the walls come crashing down.

What makes the difference between "resilient" people, who have terrible past experiences and don't react with either symptoms or problems succeeding in life? It is one of the many things that amaze me about people: how they can get tripped up and fall over and over, yet keep on going. I really believe that it is a mind-set. You can put two different people through the same set of life experiences and one will keep on going while the other is caught in the quagmire, stuck or spinning out of control. We can all learn from how these "resilient" ones dust themselves off and put their noses to the grindstone of life.

Life is not just about surviving or enduring or existing, however. It's about **living** it to its fullest, savoring and enjoying what it brings. Maybe it is about expectations of what we want out of life, what we deserve, what we feel we have earned or are entitled to. Letting the symptoms defeat us by accepting them as part of ourselves is where this vicious cycle begins. The symptoms may be a manifestation of how someone feels, but they don't have to control how they think or how they behave. One of my favorite poems, "Do Not Go Gentle into that Good Night" by Dylan Thomas begins with: "Rage, rage against the storm…", and that's what people need to do in order to battle their symptoms: don't let them win.

People who make it out of a depression challenge their lack of energy or zest for life: they go out and just do it, even if they don't feel like it. They actively work on changing the way they think about themselves and about life. Doing it makes it doable and makes them feel valued and valuable. They start to feel better about themselves and to think more positively, as if they deserve to feel better. In the same way, people who experience panic/anxiety attacks challenge themselves to do what makes them feel panicky, conquering the limitations it places on their lives. They don't let the fear of having an attack take over their lives.

It takes guts to challenge your symptoms, to take away their power over limiting your life. Making yourself sleep when you don't feel tired or wake up when you just want to sleep, pushing your nerves to their limit by ignoring feelings of panic, limiting what you eat when you just want to eat comfort food, forcing yourself to eat when you have no appetite, making yourself go out and have fun when you just don't have the energy, to concentrate when it's a chore just to wake up in the morning, never mind think. You need to take your **life** back, to enjoy it, to live it with feeling and passion, not with fear of feeling. Just **doing** makes you feel more alive, makes life more enjoyable and makes you feel more worthwhile. Now let's look at how important it is to do things for yourself and why.

Chapter 3:

The Self: Selfless or Selfish?

We have been taught that thinking of ourselves is selfish and this is simply not true. It's **not** thinking about ourselves that can lead people into trouble. Too much self-involvement is not a good thing, either. Let me explain why...

Selflessness, or thinking only about others' feelings and needs ignores a very important person: yourself. When you think only of others and don't meet, or even **know** your **own** needs, this is a recipe for disaster, both personally and for other relationships. Continually ignoring how you feel or what you want or what you need leads others to feel that you are not important. If your only happiness is through making other people happy, something is missing from your life. What about how **you** feel? If you don't know, how can you make others understand? How about what **you** want or need? If you don't know for yourself, how can others show caring for **you** and help you meet **your** needs?

Not thinking of yourself leads others to not think of you. If you don't let them know, they won't even think about it. If it's all about **them**, why should they even stop to think about you? This leads to feelings of bitterness and resentment. When you put yourself off, waiting until everyone else is happy, you do get ignored because you teach others to ignore you. They're happy and assume that you must be, too because you don't say otherwise.

Fears of being selfish often lead people to think only of others. We all know people who are self-focused, absorbed in themselves: me, me, me... Yet, they do get their needs met and their feelings heard, because they're important to themselves. It makes other people resentful of them, however, because they don't think of others. It's all about them and others run a close fourth (after me, myself, and I).

Valuing yourself is not about being selfish. You is who you live with, who you live inside of, who needs to be able to take care of you. If you don't take care of yourself, who else is going to? When all is said and done, after you have given and given and given to the point that you have nothing left for yourself, are the people you have given to even going to be aware if you haven't let them know?

I have worked with so many "givers" through the years, who come to me empty, spent, unable to give any more. Their well had run dry because nothing had filled it up, either from childhood or through the course of their lives. They had nothing more to give, either to themselves or others, and often they don't even realize it until others see them declining. A lifetime of emotional self-neglect can leave an empty shell, someone who has nothing else to give to themselves or to others.

It may seem trite, but that's where self-love comes in. Do you love and care about yourself? Do you respect yourself? Do you feel that you deserve to be cared about, to be loved, cherished, treasured, like you do others? If you don't, why not? What is the message you are giving others? You are telling them that they can take your love and caring and give nothing in return. If you don't ask for it, why should they give it? If you don't tell them what feels good, what makes you happy, what you need, how are they going to know?

I have seen many youngsters through the years whose parents describe them as "shy". They want their children to be happy, well-liked, to have friends. They want me to fix that, but if the children don't like **themselves**, how are they going to show that they are likeable? It's not always about just teaching social skills in order to help them get along well with others. They need to see themselves as worthwhile friends, someone who is fun to be with, to play with, to confide in, and to spend time with. They need to enjoy their own company, too. Self-esteem is about the **self**. It's the core word again. Teaching them to know themselves, to recognize how they feel, what they want, what they need is the beginning.

To know yourself helps you to understand others. If you know how you would be feeling or what you would be doing in a situation, it gives you an idea of how another person might feel. Understanding other people's feelings and intentions is extremely important for relationships to work. Assumptions and miscommunication interfere with how people relate if they assume the wrong feelings or intent of an action. Being able to "read" others is an extremely important skill. Assuming hurtful intent or hostility often leads to over-reactions and even more confusion between people. The admonition to "Know thyself" is an important one.

This takes us to **assertiveness**. To be assertive takes knowing yourself, how you feel, what you want and what you need. If you don't know it, how can you explain it and get it? We all have heard about passive individuals who take it and take it until they can't take it anymore. They don't tell others how they're feeling and they keep getting hurt over and over again, until they blow up. The "straw that broke the camel's back" happens and they blast someone, over-reacting from built up hurt and frustration. If they had explained how they felt, it would have told the other person what hurts and they might have stopped doing it, but piling on more and more upset leads to an explosion. At the other extreme, the aggressive individual tries to get what he or she wants and often gets it because they know what they want and go for it, whether or not it hurts someone else in the process. Neither the passive nor the aggressive approach leaves others feeling good and resentment will build up over time.

An assertive person, on the other hand, does not necessarily hurt others along the way to getting what he or she wants. She is clear with herself and in communicating with others about how she feels and what she wants or needs and works towards meeting her goal(s) in life. Assertiveness training begins with clarifying your feelings, your goals and needs and learning to communicate them to others effectively. Then, breaking down goals into more easily attainable parts makes the goals seem more realistic, not so overwhelming. Attaining the steps along the way is reinforcing and motivating, seeing yourself get closer to your goal.

So what is stopping you from getting to know yourself? Is it time? What about the time it takes to walk your dog or peel potatoes or fold laundry or work out or drive to work? What about the time you waste watching reruns or sitcoms? How about making some time you dedicate to yourself, "pencil in" during your lunch hour just for you? What are you feeling? What are you working so hard for in your relationships, at work, in life? What do you really want to do in life? If you're not happy, what would make you happy?

What would make you happier in your relationships? Are there things that bother you and you don't mention? Are there things that you enjoy doing together and you don't bother mentioning? There are things that your family and friends need to know to make you and keep you happy. Unmet needs remain unmet if they're not talked about, just like built-up resentments. I talked to one person years ago who had returned from grocery shopping, having gotten a sale on pasta (2 for 1). After she had bought the food, hauled in the groceries and was putting them all away (talk about resentments), her spouse confronted her with "Why do you always buy spaghettini, I hate spaghettini, I told you that years ago!" She was floored and more than a little upset, after having done all of the work. She didn't remember him ever having said anything about not liking that pasta, yet her spouse attributed her ignorance as hostility, never having listened to him. It's just this sort of miscommunication, of assumptions, of misperceived intentions that leads to blow-ups, hurt feelings, bitterness and resentment.

What would make you happier at work? Does everyone get along, and if not can you do something about it? Do you enjoy what you do? Are there other jobs that you'd like to learn or could already do? Do you have untapped potential that no one else there knows about? Why not tell them or request upgrading to learn more? I hear of and see so many people changing careers, feeling unfulfilled by what they are doing and I admire that immensely. It takes dedication and a strong will to go back to school and delay their futures.

It all comes down to knowing yourself. To listening to how you feel, to what makes you happy or would make you happy. To acknowledging and appreciating your own self-worth and what you want out of life. To recognizing your own needs that you need to fulfill to complete yourself. In the immortal words of Jerry

McGuire (which still bring tears to my eyes), instead of "You complete me", it should be "I complete me"! A healthy relationship starts with two intact people who can meet their own needs but also meet and complement the other's. But more about that later...

Chapter 4:

Self-Knowledge & Caring for Yourself

So we've established that it's alright (and even really important!) to consider yourself. How do you even get to know you in the first place? If you know yourself only as other people know you, there's a problem. You live inside you and they don't, so how can they know you any better? Are you listening more to others than to yourself?

We're talking here about self-discovery and self-awareness. Those thoughts running through your head? They're yours, unless you've been so pre-programmed by others' voices (parents, peers, teachers, coaches, bosses, etc.) to simply repeat the same. How would you even know that? Well...if you close your eyes and just let then flow through (especially any negative ones), pause and listen to whose voice it is saying them. It may just be that you've been so used to hearing and accepting what others say about you that you've simply come to accept it.

Some people find journaling a great way to really get to know themselves. It's simply taking a little time in a quiet place without distractions to think about life and writing about it. It's basically keeping a diary of just about anything: how your day went, how you feel, what things bothered you, what things felt great, how you thought through and worked through things. As much as journaling allows you to get to know yourself better, understanding your thoughts and feelings, it can also help with stress-reduction by letting go of intense feelings as you write about them. It lets you be heard, to express your perspective.

If the thought of writing to and about yourself on a regular or semi-regular basis (remember, it doesn't have to be every day) just doesn't fit, then consider meditation. Meditating promotes calming and relaxation, which is a tremendous benefit, even of itself. Many find that the inner peace and serenity they experience creates a tremendous sense of well-being. It is all about directing one's attention and awareness inward, becoming mindful. The health and mental health benefits of mindful meditation have been well documented.

While meditation can be all about self-discovery, it is also about *self-care*. The health and mental health benefits of mindful meditation have been and continue to be well-documented. So how do you care for yourself? What do you do for you that takes care of your needs? (Notice that the focus on self-discovery may even uncover other needs that haven't been met.)

Of course there are the basic needs for survival like eating, drinking, maintaining proper hygiene and healthcare, getting enough sleep, etc., but what else do you do for yourself to nurture you? For instance, hygiene includes regular showers or baths, but do you really love a long, relaxing, soaking bubble bath and never seem to have the time to take one? What stops you from making time? Eating is for the purpose of providing your body energy, but do you find yourself simply grabbing something quick instead of making something special for yourself that you really enjoy eating? Everyone needs regular nightly sleep, but do you really love a luxurious nap on a day off? What stops you?

Yes, time gets in the way of so many things we want to do, but in that busy schedule of so much to do for work, for family, etc., where have you scheduled in time for yourself? No one else is going to, so why not do it for yourself?

We're talking here about not just *physical* self-care, but also *emotional, social* and *spiritual.* These are all parts of ourselves that need to be nurtured. When I mention *emotional* health and self-care, the focus is on emotional needs like love, feeling cared about, and dealing with negative emotions like fear, anxiety, anger, frustration, sadness, etc. How do you deal with these emotions? Do you reach out to others for empathy and understanding? Do you try to cope with them by yourself? If so, how is that working for you?

What helps you cope with negative emotions on your own? If you just ignore them or let them fester inside, that's never good. That's called *internalization* and it's like an infection that grows unchecked, damaging the healthy parts of the body. If you *externalize* them, taking them out on other people, that's not good for the other people in your life. If you have healthier ways of dealing with them, like through exercise and activities, at least that's helping you let go of the physical side of pent-up emotions.

Why not reach out to others for their support? Everyone needs someone sometimes. It can really help to talk things through with a trusted friend or family member to get their perspective and empathy. They may not be able to solve any problems, but it can feel a lot better to share what's going on with you. That's why we're social beings.

Abraham Maslow, a psychologist, wrote about what he saw as a hierarchy of 5 basic needs (physical, safety, social, esteem and actualization) back in the 1940's and 1950's. We've already talked about the physical needs and I see safety needs as part of the emotional and social needs. Maslow defined them as the need for love, intimacy family, friends, and a sense of belonging.

Now let's look at *social* needs, which are closely tied in with emotional needs. Not everyone is a social butterfly, and each person is different in terms of their desire and needs to be around others. We do need to feel loved, otherwise people wouldn't search so hard for a partner in life or feel so hurt if they haven't felt the love of their parents or caregivers growing up. That also ties into the need to feel a sense of belonging, whether to a family of origin, a family they've created, or someplace with others with similar interests.

Do you feel loved by someone? If not, do you feel that someone cares about you or have you been so hurt that you've closed yourself off from fear of being hurt again? Have you given up trying and just settled on life on your own or are you still searching? All I can say is open yourself up to the possibility of letting others into your life. Sure, you may get hurt again, but think about the possibilities!

If you've felt that every time you open yourself up to others, they disappoint you, then really think about the people you've been reaching out to. What have they had in common? If you can figure that out, then look for different people who are more likely to be good for you. To be able to trust someone and feel accepted is a really big thing towards self-acceptance. Try again.

Being around others promotes a sense of self-esteem, feeling respected and building self-respect. We're not talking about having such a huge ego that your big head can't make it through a door. We're talking about feeling good about yourself, your achievements and accomplishments, whatever they may be. Everyone deserves that.

Now let's talk about *spiritual* needs, which don't have to be in the religious sense, but they can be. Here, we're talking about activities that nurture your soul and contribute to mental health. That can include prayer, meditation, anything that promotes a sense of inner peace and well-being. For some, that includes regular attendance at a place of worship. For others, they search out and find that place inside them, wherever they are. It could be at the top of a mountain they've climbed, where they stand in awe, marveling at the beauty of the world around them. For some it could be as easy as quietly sitting in their favorite chair, letting the memories of positive, affirming life experiences flow through their minds.

Self-care promotes good health, happiness and overall well-being. Are there any better reasons not to practice it? Even if you can't justify doing it for yourself (and you should!), remind yourself that you're a role-model for your kids and your spouse. If they don't see you taking care of or caring about yourself, why should they care about or consider you? Don't you want your children to consider and take care of themselves in their futures? These are good habits for you and them to learn and practice as part of daily life.

Chapter 5:

Habits: We All Have Them, Good and Bad

A habit is defined as a repetitive behavior that is frequently done without thinking or conscious awareness. When people think of habits, they most often think of doing things that are bad for them, like drinking excessively, or smoking, or biting their nails. Yet, we all have many habits that we do on a daily basis that are good for us, like brushing our teeth, or checking in the rear-view mirror before a lane change, or checking that the iron is off before we leave the house. These and many others are adaptive and we often do them without even thinking.

Negative habits are always the focus of needing help with getting rid of or replacing them. They serve a function too, however and are often a coping strategy to deal with uncomfortable feelings. Take drinking, for example. Some people drink in a social situation because it's what everyone else is doing. Others drink in social situations to make themselves feel less anxious, less inhibited or more relaxed. They cope with these feelings by masking them to feel more comfortable. Some people drink excessively to help them forget how they're feeling in general. They do so socially or on their own, trying to make themselves feel better, but feel worse in the end because the feelings return and they end up with a hangover, to boot. The same goes for drug abuse. The focus of growth needs to be on understanding and dealing with the underlying reasons and feelings that drive the habit. It's one thing to abstain, and in so doing, avoid social situations and the stressors that lead to drinking. It's another to learn to cope with these feelings in healthier ways and reduce the build-up of negative emotions by letting go of the past.

As well as the obvious health and relationship concerns with excessive drinking, there is the lack of emotional growth that happens. Let me explain. I spoke to a wise person many years ago who had worked with someone who had been a huge drinker for much of her life. He explained that the individual had been clean and sober for several years. The person was in her sixties at the time and had started drinking in her late teens. She said she figured that she was emotionally just hitting her twenties. As she explained it, she felt that she had not learned to deal with anything with a clear head for all those years, drinking to avoid the feelings and situations that made her feel bad. She had not grown by experiencing and working through issues throughout life. We learn by experiencing failure, growing by making mistakes. I learned a lot and have been able to share what was taught to me with others who use alcohol to excess.

Habits are driven by many different emotions. Take nail-biting, for example. It's a clear sign of anxiety, stress, or inner tension. Most often, this habit starts in childhood. Again, simply stopping the behavior by punishment does not deal with what drives it. The person is still left with overwhelming emotions and nowhere to channel them. One needs to understand what the feelings and experiences are that trigger it. For instance, does it happen in performance or testing situations? Does it happen at home, when there's conflict going on? Does it happen in social situations where the person feels uncomfortable? Does it happen absent-mindedly when a person is thinking about past situations?

Being able to pin-point what a person is thinking about or what is happening when they do it allows for some degree of control through predictability. To know why you're doing it is the first step. The next step is learning to deal with the emotions or situations more effectively, in healthier ways to build up the confidence and feel less tense or anxious. If it happens in social situations, don't avoid them, approach them, rehearse and practice learning social skills. If it happens in performance situations, prepare for them more to feel confident and learn relaxation skills. If it happens when conflict is happening at home and you're not involved in it, leave or get occupied with something else.

Anxiety and tension are the opposite of feeling relaxed. It's really hard to feel stressed when your body is in a relaxed state. Why else do people go on holidays? Other than to experience a new place, a lot of holidays are booked to get away from everyday stresses and worries, to feel free, away from it all. Can anyone feel tense relaxing on a beach watching the waves or floating on an air mattress in a hotel pool? (Unless of course they can't swim or have a phobia of sea-birds). Everyone has their ideal place to escape to, whether it's out to the mountains or a day at a spa or going on a tropical holiday. But where to find that inner sense of peace on a daily basis?

There are so many ways of promoting relaxation and letting go of tension and anxiety. It's different for everyone. I know that for me, swimming works like a charm. I just have to start my laps, focusing on each stroke and the feeling of the water, exerting myself as far as I can take it, and I leave feeling so much better.

Similarly, working out at my gym, doing cardio on the treadmill and focusing on each step, my breath and heartbeat, then pushing myself on each machine, focusing on each muscle leaves me feeling energized and exhausted at the same time. Walking my dog, watching him make friends as he runs in the green space behind my house makes him feel good and me, too. Pets are extremely relaxing. You can just feel your tension drain out as you sit with a cat on your lap purring as you pet him or her. Even watching your fish in an aquarium is a great tension-reducer. Why do you think doctors and dentists frequently have aquariums in their waiting rooms?

Even hobbies are healthy habits, releases for people, something to look forward to at the end of a long day. Having a passion for sewing or doing crafts or knitting or bowling or building models or cooking or baking, for ballroom-dancing or playing softball or soccer or bike-riding or racing cars or riding motorcycles all have something in common: they make us feel good. They promote relaxation and are often a great source of self-esteem. Have you ever envied someone who makes their hobby, their passion into a career? They get to do what they want and make money at it. Whether it's a career or not, however, people with hobbies know that they have something they enjoy, that makes them feel happy.

There are so many other ways to channel negative emotions, positive habits to switch to when they come up. Understanding what triggers unhealthy habits gives you some control over them. Learning more successful, confidence-building, less anxiety-inducing ways to handle situations reduces the need for the habit. When tension or anxiety does build up, having positive outlets to turn to in order to promote feelings of calm, relaxation, and well-being are like a "pill in your pocket", always there when you need them.

Chapter 6:

What has Anxiety/Pain/Sadness ever done for me?

When someone goes to see their family doctor other than for a check-up, it's because of an ache, a pain, some discomfort that is bothering them. They have a physical warning sign that something may be wrong. A fever is usually a sign that the body is fighting some sort of infection, a rash or hives may be an allergic reaction. If our physical inner state feels unbalanced, "out-of-sync" or uncomfortable, we know it. From experience living in our bodies, we know when something is wrong or different and if it's troublesome enough, we seek medical attention.

Just as a person has the body awareness to know when it just doesn't feel right, when a cold lasts too long or a fever gets too high or an ache becomes a persistent sharp pain, there is also an emotional equilibrium within each of us. All people have an ebb and flow, ups and downs, some higher and lower than others, but we have a self-awareness when things feel "unbalanced", when we feel "out-of-sorts". Our internal emotional warning signs are persistent anxiety, intense emotional pain and prolonged sadness.

Anxiety is part of the fight-or-flight response. When we feel anxious, our mind is telling us that there is something troubling us, whether it's triggered by an external event, like an upcoming test, or an internal event, like a memory. Anxiety heightens our awareness, puts us in defensive mode. If it's something we can control, like studying more for a test or preparing for a confrontation, it serves a purpose by motivating us to reduce the anxiety. If it's something out of our control, like a recurring memory triggered by similar experiences like visiting a hospital where some we love has died before, it only serves as a constant reminder of a traumatic experience.

People who suffer from Post-Traumatic Stress Disorder experience persistent anxiety and frequently terror in situations that remind them of the traumatic event. For instance, if a person has been held hostage in a bank, a life-threatening situation, he or she may have a panic reaction just driving by a bank. A person who has been attacked in the dark out for a walk at night may become afraid of the dark or hyper-vigilant (extremely sensitive) to noises or panic-stricken if someone comes up behind them unexpectedly. These are reminders or warning signs of a terrifying event that still carries with them an extreme amount of negative emotion. Even a smell, a sound, a taste that reminds them of it can trigger it. It's not even just external events that are a trigger. Experiencing a similar emotion, even just a hint of upset or anxiety can also trigger these post-traumatic reactions.

Anxiety is a strong internal warning sign that something doesn't feel right. People may experience anxiety in different ways: some have chest pains or feel their hearts beating faster, some experience rapid breathing or profuse sweating, some shake, some just feel shaky or tense, and some feel antsy inside. It doesn't necessarily take a traumatic experience to feel anxiety, however it manifests itself for each of us. Persistent anxiety that generalizes, or spreads into much of a person's life can be very debilitating as it is a drain on the system, exhausting the body with adrenaline rushes. It can also hamper people from trying new experiences or even old ones. Social anxiety happens when people are afraid to make themselves appear stupid out in public by saying or doing the wrong thing. They may become increasingly uncomfortable in social situations and start to avoid them. Performance anxiety occurs when someone is afraid to fail in a performance or testing situation. It may increase to the extent that they avoid performance situations, whether it's acting, playing music, playing a sport, or writing tests.

There is nothing wrong with some anxiety. It keeps us on our toes if it's in moderation. I have heard many famous athletes and performing artists say that they still feel butterflies in their stomachs before the show or the game, even after years at it. It's what they do with the anxiety, letting it flow to motivate them, to approach the situation and not avoid it, that makes the difference. Too much anxiety can narrow a person's life to the point that they avoid anything that makes them feel anxious.

Anxiety, like emotional pain or sadness, tells us that something is bothering us. If we continue to endure it and over time it doesn't lessen or go away, it makes our lives less enjoyable. In fact, it makes it plain miserable awaiting the next situation or memory that is going to bring up anxiety and other negative feelings. It's not as easy as just saying to yourself: "Just don't think about...", because in thinking that, you think about the memory. I use this analogy with people: "Don't think of pink elephants"...what picture comes up in your mind but pink elephants dancing around like in the movie Fantasia?

I really believe that guilt can be a very damaging emotion. Excessive guilt or self-blame can sap a person of the strength and energy to deal with a situation. A realistic amount of guilt can be necessary to take responsibility for a wrongdoing or inaction. Experiencing guilt can be motivating to make changes, to ensure that the same outcome doesn't happen again, but too much can be paralyzing.

The opposite side of the coin is blame. Of course, it puts the person being blamed on the defensive. If that other person is truly responsible for whatever it is, that is one thing, but if they're not and the act of blaming another is to rid the blamer of guilt, that's never good. It doesn't help them grow and potentially does damage to the relationship. I often look at it this way: there are 3 sides to every story. One is the first person's perspective, two is the other person's perspective and three is what really happened (or the truth is somewhere in-between the first two). Again, it's all about balance: too much guilt isn't good, nor is too much blame.

Thoughts and memories are emotionally-charged. There's a basic tenet of many therapies that states that thoughts lead to feelings which lead to behaviors. Let me explain this further, because it's very important.

Think of anything: an experience, a memory, a future event, a person. You have some feeling about it, right? Based on that feeling, people act in some way towards that experience, either reliving it, approaching it, or avoiding it. Let's take several examples. Let's say you remember your first date ever and it was a good one. You feel happy remembering that positive experience and are then more likely to repeat the behavior. If you remember it as a negative experience, you feel bad or embarrassed or any other negative emotion and are less likely to want to repeat the behavior, perhaps to the extent of avoiding dating altogether.

There can be what I call a "spiraling effect", a positive upward spiral and a negative downward spiral. Let's take that same dating scenario with someone having a good first experience, feeling good about it and being willing to date again. I'm being simplistic here, but humor me. That experience can also generalize or extend to how they feel about themselves, improving their self-esteem, increasing their self-confidence, making them more positive about dating again, more productive at work, at home, having positive thoughts about challenges ahead of them. If we take the negative scenario with the bad experience, the person could think all dates will go that way, feeling bad about him or herself and would be less likely to date again, expecting another negative experience. This can generalize or extend into a downward spiral of negative thinking, feeling less desirable, with lowered confidence, poor self-esteem and less likelihood of approaching new challenges in all areas of his or her life. You can see how multiple negative early experiences can have a snow-balling effect.

This process is a two-way street and that's what we use to help people in therapy: behaviors also lead to feelings which lead to thoughts. In other words, by doing something, we have some feeling about the experience and think about it in a certain way. Let's say a person has never ridden a horse before, they ride and feel good about it, which makes them think they want to do it again. Therapy works from both directions in that working towards changing thoughts and behaviors can change the feelings. I like to work in both directions, essentially attacking the negative emotions from both directions. I'll explain how this works with several scenarios.

Let's say a person has just been refused a promotion or a raise at work and feels badly about him or herself, thinking they must be unworthy. He or she can either blame it on the boss (taking it personally, that they're cheap or ungrateful), on the company (they don't recognize or reward good work), on the economy (times are tough and maybe the company isn't doing well), or on themselves (maybe they aren't doing as well as they thought, there's something about them that makes them unworthy). A person can't help but feel bad about the situation, but if they take it personally, thinking it's something they're not doing right or enough of, it can reduce their motivation at work, their drive to succeed.

A positive spin on the situation would be to work harder or get more innovative, perhaps while looking elsewhere in the job market if they have don't have confidence in the boss or the company. A negative spin would make them lose their drive, working less productively because "it doesn't matter what I do anyway, no one recognizes it". This would only reinforce the negative feelings, resulting in reduced achievement motivation, feelings of hopelessness and powerlessness. Those same feelings could also impact on other areas of their lives, as in their relationships (feeling too down or unsuccessful to date), and their free time (no energy or desire to go out or do hobbies or activities that make them feel better).

How to undo the damage of negative life experiences or failures on the future? First of all, you need to do a clear appraisal of what happened, after the initial shock and disappointment of the experience has subsided. Any negative experience can involve feelings of loss and entails a grieving process, with the first stage being disbelief. Is it really due to something you did or didn't do? You're angry and upset, but is there anything you could have done differently that would have changed the outcome?

This brings us to *resilience*. Resilient people seem to make it through tough life experiences and come out the other side okay, sometimes even better. How can it be that the same negative experience can cause some people to falter and get stuck in their misery for years while others seem to take it in their stride? That's not saying that the experiences haven't changed them, it's just that they somehow adapt. The ability to be resilient is not extraordinary. People do it all the time. They've suffered through, experienced the gamut of negative emotions like everyone else, but have developed ways to make it through and past.

Resilient people reach out to others for support, whether it's family members or caring, reassuring friends who they feel they can unconditionally trust.

How they view the world makes a difference. They've developed their own coping strategies in times of stress.

There is no one way to be resilient, but there are similarities found in people who adjust well to difficult life experiences. As I already mentioned, people who exhibit resiliency experience the strong emotions like everyone in response to a negative life experience. The difference is that they don't let the emotions take over and control them. They reach out to others and are able to take a step back from experiencing them at times when they need to.

There is also a common way they view the world, a more positive, optimistic view in general. This extends to how they view themselves, as well. They are confident that they can and will make it through, confident in their ability to succeed and be happy again. They have hope that things will get better and this motivates them to keep moving forward.

When it comes to difficult life experiences, resilient people don't just wish it had never happened (although they do that, as well). They try to actively deal with it, doing something towards resolution. It is a problem that must be solved (although the event can't be changed), and they address it, one step at a time.

There is an attitude and set of beliefs that resilient people embrace. They believe they will overcome the experience. They come to expect and acknowledge that change will happen in life, instead of dreading it. They believe that they can grow and learn something about themselves from the experience.

Even through it all, people who display resilience still keep some positive momentum, moving forward and directing their attention (even a bit, as much as they can) on the future and what they want to accomplish. Connecting with others is a big part of that and many people who display resilience reach out to help others, as they find that helping others also helps them feel better, more useful and allows them to regain perspective.

Resilient people know what has worked for them in the past in order to cope with and make it through stressful life experiences. If those coping strategies don't work for them again, they take that problem-solving approach to figure out another way, whether on their own or with the help of others. They do not shy away from reaching out to others for help when they know they need it.

Finally, people who display resilience ensure that they take care of themselves. They pay attention to their physical, emotional, social, and spiritual needs. Neglecting any of them can lead to imbalance. They give themselves time to relax, to do things they enjoy doing, whatever it may be. They nurture themselves, which is so important to the rebuilding process.

Chapter 7:

Your Inner Voice: Whose is it and what is it telling you?

We all have a running patter that plays in our heads, a stream of conscious thought that we use to explain what goes on around us. This is what I call our inner voice. It comes from our own life experiences and what we have been told about ourselves or others throughout our lives. I describe it as being like a player piano roll that repeats itself over and over. Some people tend to think positive thoughts about themselves and others. Other people's inner voice can be a very negative one and they automatically say or think negative things about themselves and others without even realizing it. This is a very simplistic dichotomy of course, like the "glass half-full/glass half-empty" image, but let's follow it further...

When someone tells me only negative things about him or herself, I often have them shut their eyes and listen to what their thoughts are telling them...whose voice is it, their own or someone else's? More times than not, it is the voice of a negative person in their lives: a parent, a family member, a teacher, a coach. They are shocked and dismayed that they have internalized what others have told them so strongly that it colors their lives.

Think about it...what do you think to yourself about things that you do or see others do? Do you automatically cheer yourself on, saying "good job, I knew I could do it", or do you think to yourself: "I should have been able to that better, I never do things right"? Think back to the major figures in your life, the important people who helped you become who you are...what did they tell you about yourself? Did they give you messages like in the book "The Little Engine That Could" (which, by the way has been touted as the major positive motivational book of the 20th century)? Or did they tell you that you were "never good enough, would never amount to anything"? Imagine how continuously hearing these different messages about yourself would impact on your motivation, how you see yourself, how hard you'd try to succeed.

Similarly, think about what you were told about other people...were they to be cheered on and complimented (like many coaches do with kids on teams..."nice try!"), or were they put down at others' expense ("who does she think she is dressed like that?")? Maybe it's due to the survival of the species, but I find women, starting in their teen years as brutal in how they treat each other.

The put-downs (especially behind other girls' backs) are damaging to self-esteem and often can last a life-time. Even now, if you watch adult women in bars and night-clubs, they are constantly making comparisons of other women's dress, hairstyles and make-up. That's an over-generalization, because not all women do it, but look at how much more elaborately women tend to dress to go out than their male counter-parts. When I say survival of the species, I mean it may have been adaptive in the days when finding and attracting a mate was our sole purpose, but it's not that way anymore. But I digress...

Bullies, a huge problem in the schoolyard right on up to the corporate world, either verbally or physically attack others to make themselves feel better. In their insecurity about themselves, they make others feel bad in order to make themselves feel good. Judging others negatively and putting them down, even covertly, on a constant basis wastes energy that could be better spent on yourself. Think about it...how does it help to think badly of others? Why not work on making yourself better?

When I'm trying to help someone motivate themselves to succeed, I would much rather have them compare themselves to **themselves**! Improving your own performance relative to before just makes more sense...no one else has your same capabilities or understands you more than you do, so why not focus on being a better you? When I worked with school children, I didn't have them focus on others' marks or performance, I taught them to focus on improving their **own** effort, study habits, work habits, and "self-statements".

What you say to yourself about you and others makes a huge difference in self-esteem, drive and motivation, as well as relationships. There's a line I love from one of Adam Sandler's movies with a character whose sole purpose in the movie is to say (with a funny accent)..."you can do it!" and I can't help but think of that line, which I use with my own kids all the time. It sticks with you, like the little engine ("I think I can, I think I can...").

We live inside ourselves and can be our best cheerleaders or our own worst enemies and for this reason, we need to be good to ourselves. Even if bad habits or patterns have been established that make us naturally think bad things about ourselves or others, these patterns can be changed with awareness and with effort. Remember, it's easier to keep up old ways, even if they don't make us feel good, because they're effortless and we don't even realize we're doing it. So the next time you catch yourself thinking something negative about yourself, *give your head a shake* and think or say something **good**...remember you're your own coach and the best ones motivate their players to keep trying, to feel good about themselves, and not to give up!

Chapter 8:

The 4 Cornerstones of a Healthy Relationship

In my work with couples, I found that they most often came for therapy at the 10- and 20-year mark of being together. At ten years into a relationship, they most often have a child or children together and are beginning to lose themselves as individuals and as a couple. Many stay together "for the children", but have not allowed themselves to continue to grow as individuals or together as a couple. They are missing some critical components of what they needed to keep on doing. The 20-year point is often when the children are starting to leave home and the empty-nesters look at each other across the dinner table, wondering: "who are you, other than mom or dad?". Unfortunately, sometimes things are too far gone to find themselves again as individuals within the relationship or as a couple to repair what they have lost. Luckily, often there is enough love and dedication there to have a solid foundation to work on together again. It takes a lot of patience and compassion to help each other find their way. I felt truly blessed when I had the trust of these people to help them find themselves again.

Communication, honesty, respect and trust...those are the four components that make or break a relationship. It's as simple as that. If a couple had them at one time, they can regain them, but without regular maintenance and nurturance of each other, they start to disintegrate. Any inequities between two people, whether it's in a marriage, between parent and child, between children, between adult siblings, friends, and co-workers or between children and authority figures, the imbalance causes problems. It takes recognition, caring and effort to maintain a healthy relationship. Let's look at how this "relationship box", with the components at the four corners keeping it strong and symmetrical is supposed to work. There has to be a balance between partners in a relationship on all 4 components, as well as stability within the relationship over time.

In order to begin a relationship with someone, there has to be **communication** or you would never have met in the first place. Communication is the sharing of ideas, feelings, thoughts, memories, and experiences, among other things. It can be verbal or non-verbal, through body language or facial expression. Think of when you met your significant other for the first time. How did you connect? What did you talk about? What did you get to know about them or what did they get to know about you in the beginning? How long did it take to really "get to know" each other? How much did you share about yourself?

Keeping up with communication/sharing is a never-ending process. Does anyone ever really know everything about us? Do they need to? Without proper, honest talk, miscommunication and assumptions arise that can lead to hurt, anger and built-up resentment. Years of not really listening, but filtering another person's words through our own needs and perspectives lead to detachment from each other. Why bother talking when it feels like no one is listening? The balance between talking and listening has to be maintained. More about communication later...

Honesty begins from the first communication with each other. It's about saying what we truly feel, what we really think, who we really are. First impressions count, and sometimes people "stretch the truth" in the beginning of a relationship in order to attract the other person (or not detract from themselves). This is to be expected, but to be a genuine person with someone else is to be the person you present yourself to be. Some of this depends upon where two people meet. If it's in a bar, chances are that the initial attraction is not to the person inside, because that's not what they see.

If it lasts past the first flurry, it takes time to get to know someone. Relationships that start through work or mutual interests tend to give a clearer picture of the other person, that there are things in common already.

Does honesty mean sharing every nitty-gritty detail about our lives? Some people feel that some of their past is better left unsaid and could be perceived as "baggage" by the other person. Our past experiences have shaped and contributed to who we are, however, and would help explain how we feel and what we do. Whereas being honest, or telling the truth about the past (which may come out anyway and result in feelings of betrayal if it comes from somewhere else) may depend upon how much the other person wants to hear, honesty about **feelings** is of paramount importance. There is no question that some people talk more from their heads than from their hearts, and when paired with each other, this mix of the two can spell disaster. If the heart/feelings person tries to express how they feel and it is intellectualized by the head/thoughts person, it can lead to serious feelings of being misunderstood. They almost speak in two different languages and practically need a translator.

Talking about what feels good that the other person is doing or has done, as well as what doesn't feel so good helps a relationship immeasurably. If this doesn't happen, resentments will build up. How else is your partner to know what you want or need (or don't want or need)? No one is a mind-reader. Assuming that the other person knows or **should** know only sets you both up for failure. Spell it out, explain it clearly and be patient. Be open to feedback and discussion but don't just sit there and let things repeat themselves, digging wounds deeper. Don't forget to be appreciative and mention the things they do that feel great. We all have a tendency to take for granted the good things and focus on the bad. Think about it: if you do something for someone and they're really appreciative and grateful for it (and you care about them), aren't you going to want to do that again? Of course you are!

Respect is such a misunderstood word. It means something different to everyone. When I worked with teens and their parents, the word came up constantly in that both want to be respected. In questioning further, however, it is often clear that it means different things to each of them. To parents, often respect means following the rules, no swearing or yelling at them, and no name-calling. To teens, it often means giving them their privacy: not snooping in their email or phone messages, not reading their diaries or going into their rooms without asking first. They're using the same word to describe two different but complementary needs. The same goes for any relationship.

This is where we see the other components inter-play. In order to have our needs respected, we have to effectively **communicate** them to the other person. We also have to be **honest** about how things make us feel so that we don't "set up" the other person to disrespect the needs we haven't effectively communicated. Respect is mutual in that there has to be a balance. People will respect those who they feel respect them.

We live in a different era than when I grew up, as like many of us, I was raised to "respect my elders" unconditionally, even if I felt that sometimes they didn't respect me. Giving people respect was unquestioned back then, yet I continually hear from many teenagers that they'll give their parents when they feel they're respected, not unconditionally. The same goes for other authority figures in their lives, like teachers: we were taught at home that we should respect our teachers and listen to what they wanted from us without question. The "earning respect" motto seems to have extended to kids in the classroom nowadays, because I have never seen more defiance of teachers ever. This creates its own share of problems. In any case, in any relationship, both parties need to feel respected by the other, to feel valued and worthy of being treated well. Any imbalance will cause resentment.

Finally, the fourth cornerstone of a healthy relationship is **trust**. Can we trust the other person's feelings, their intentions, and their honesty? Can they be depended upon? This depends upon where a person comes from in previous relationships. If they've been lied to or cheated on, they're less likely to be trusting from the beginning. People come from different directions on this one. Some people give all of their trust in the beginning, "laying their cards on the table", "putting their hearts on their sleeve" and hoping that the other person also "bargains in good faith". Others feel that trust has to be earned and slowly share how they feel, what they've experienced, what they want and need. It's a slower process for them to "test the waters", to let the other person prove that they are worthy of greater trust.

Some would consider the first person, who gives trust unquestioningly, to be naïve. Yet, they are willing to take a chance and show "all of their cards", who they really are from the beginning because they believe that if they don't show you who they really are, they may attract the wrong person. They take a big chance of being hurt. The second, more cautious individual is wary of being hurt and often feels that trust, like respect, has to be earned. While they may be less likely to be hurt earlier on in a relationship because they take their time to get to know someone and to show who they are, they may lose out as well. Who they show themselves to be may not attract the right person from the beginning and they may set themselves up for failure.

Any way you look at it, relationships are incredibly complex. There is so much going on, of what people are willing to show of themselves: what they want, what they need, how they feel, what they've been through. Communication is the key to being honest, to being able to trust and be trusted, to being respected. Love is only the beginning...

Chapter 9:

Our Family Tree: Watching it Grow

The decision to have children is a selfish one. They don't ask to be here, we just make them. I really like the words to one of the latest country songs that says: "Any fool can make a baby, but it takes a man to raise a child" (Chris Young, 2011), because it encompasses all the worries, the anguish, the frustrations, the attention, the joys and thrills of being a parent.

I remember when my own two children were born, the pure joy of holding them and marveling at their existence, but I also remember the sadness I felt for them in the buzzing confusion of this world, unprotected by the peaceful sanctuary of the womb. How scary it must be to suddenly be out here, bombarded by noises, sights, smells and everything they can't even begin to comprehend. I marvel at nature's way of pre-wiring babies to know our voices from day 1, having been attuned to them from hearing them inside. They recognize us and trust us implicitly to take care of them, to meet their needs. Their focal length at birth, where they can see best is almost exactly at the distance from their tiny faces to ours when they suckle at our breast or the bottle and they gaze at us as we gaze back, innocent and beguiling. What a huge responsibility to hold a life in our hands and guide it, nurture it, shape it to survive, to grow and mature. Their very existence changes our focus from ourselves and meeting our own needs to another human life totally reliant upon us. What a treasure, a gift that gives back so much more than we can possibly realize.

Before pregnancy, we ate what we wanted to or when we wanted to, slept when we wanted to, did what we wanted or needed to in order to fulfill our own needs (or not). With pregnancy, what we eat or the sleep we get or the exertion we do affects the growing baby and the focus needs to change to consider them, safe and protected away from the world. What we put into or do with our bodies goes into them...their growth, their heartbeat, their circulation, their development.

With their arrival into our world, there are so many other factors that we can't control...other people, their friends, the media, and their teachers, among so many others. All that we can do is provide the most love, the best nutrition, the right amount of sleep, the most loving care-givers, the safest environment, the most positive attention and focus on their physical, social, emotional and spiritual growth. I always tell young expectant parents that if they can give their babies all the love, all the confidence in themselves they can, it will help to shelter them from all the negatives in the world around us. They will be able to trust us to care for and about them and to trust themselves.

I read a poem once about how children come to us like packets of seeds that we plant, water and watch them grow and flower. We don't necessarily know what they will turn out like, all we can do is provide the best soil, the right amount of sunlight and water to help them thrive. It's truly that way with our children. We don't know what they're going to look like, sound like, act like, who they will be as they grow. We don't know the genetic combinations that make them who they are among the billions of possible combinations. In the beginning, all we can do is nurture who they come to us as and try to understand them. They will teach us as we learn and grow at the same time.

Parents are made in the process of raising their children. They are not born, but mature and develop because they have to in order to adapt. Children do not come with operating instructions. We have to figure it out from our own experiences being parented and from who our children are as individuals. There is no cookbook, no menu, no recipe for raising a child successfully, we make it up as we go along. We take what we have been taught by our experience and adjust by what worked, what didn't, what made us feel good, what made us feel bad. We adjust by who the child is, how they act, how they feel, what they show us, what they tell us in words, and by their behavior. Each child has a different temperament, a different way of reacting, of understanding, of seeing, of feeling and interpreting. The same strategies may not work with the next child because they are a completely different person. We ask advice from our parents or our friends who are already parents, but the bottom line is they are not our children's parents. They have not parented our child or children and don't know them like we do.

The bond is the first connection with a child. Every baby looks beautiful to their parents and don't tell them anything different! Even though first-time parents have never been bonded to their own child before, they have hopefully experienced the parent-child bond from the other direction. There's nothing like it and it's so powerful, yet indescribable in words unless you've experienced it yourself. To know that you've brought this little person into the world and they depend upon you so completely, so totally, so unquestioningly to survive and to love them is an overwhelming feeling.

We show the infant love by caring about them, trying to meet their every need. We try to anticipate what they need, and their cries are their communication to us. Parents learn to interpret the cries: do they need food, a diaper change, a cuddle, are they in pain? There are many interpretations and differing advice on responding to an infant's cries. Some say that picking them up at every cry creates a spoiled child who just has to whimper to get attention. From my own experience, I never could just close the door and let my babies cry, either of them. I was lucky enough that neither child was a colicky baby and they didn't cry non-stop, but I felt that if they were making the effort to say something, even if it meant "I'm bored, come play with me", why would I want to miss that opportunity? Relationships are about trust and if a child doesn't know that they can trust their parent to acknowledge them and respond, how sad must it feel to be crying their little hearts out and the door gets closed to avoid their noise?

The newborn phase is exhausting as they are so helpless, so dependent upon us to survive in every way. Who can ever forget each and every new accomplishment, from the first smile (they know me and they're happy!) to the first time they coo and roll over, when they start to reach for things, play with their toes, babble and chatter, start to crawl, then stand up, couch-surf, then take their first steps. Each and every new change makes them more individual, more autonomous as they start to express their own little personality. It is also the beginning of their separation from and growth away from us.

Chapter 10:

Our Family Tree: The Preschool Years

I'll never understand why it's called the "terrible twos", other than the fact that by that age, most toddlers are mobile, talking, and starting to become more independent. They aren't just doing what they're told anymore and are beginning to say "no" at times to what they're asked or told. Some tantrums may have started in their frustration at getting their needs met or their feelings understood, but why is that so terrible? Don't get me wrong, a tantrum in a grocery store because a child wants a certain candy or sugary cereal should not be appeased (why do they put that stuff at kiddie eye-level?) to stop the tantrum. If they don't stop the antics, you need to remove them from the store. But many tantrums are a toddler's attempt at trying to express a multitude of emotions and they either can't recognize them or say them in words. Patience and gentle coaching by asking how they feel or suggesting what their faces tell us about how they feel can many times alleviate the frustration at feeling misunderstood. They are becoming more of their own person with real people feelings, interpretations, intentions, assumptions, miscommunications and frustrations. But they are certainly less controllable than a babe-in-arms. I always felt that this stage was more exciting, watching how their minds worked to try and understand, to problem-solve and express themselves. We finally have a window on their minds that we could only hope to interpret before they could go where they wanted to go and start to say what they want or how they feel.

How we deal with this new-found autonomy and independence is crucial. Do we ignore what they're trying to tell us and tell them how they should feel? Do we get angry and punish their frustrations? If we do, that may be the beginning of a child learning that their feelings are either wrong or don't matter. Do we take the time to listen and help them put their feelings into words, to understand that not every want is a need?

The pre-school stage is such a formative one as children absorb what we say and what we do, like little sponges. We are their gurus as they ask the most amazing questions and expect us to know all of the answers. ("Why is the sky blue? How far away is heaven? Why is grass green? Why do dogs have tails?.") Just ask a parent of a teenager who has suddenly become the stupidest person in their teenager's life ("You just don't get it, you don't understand...") how much they miss it, but more about that later...

We start watching our preschoolers interact with other children in daycares or day-homes, in play-groups or play-schools or parks. They learn that they have to share and how to share, to listen to other children and how they feel, to read their emotions by body-language and facial expressions, to express themselves and be listened to, as well. I believe that learning these skills is as important, if not more important than the pre-school drawing, writing, and pre-reading skills like learning the alphabet. Don't get me wrong, for a child to enter kindergarten and not know their ABC's and 123's or how to color or have the fine-motor skills to cut around shapes puts them behind their age-mates, and we have to encourage them to make learning fun, to set them up for success. But at the same time, school is not only academic, it's social as well. And schools/educators recognize that. If you look at report cards, not only are their grades or numbers for academic performance, but also ratings for social/emotional development ("needs improvement" to "excellent"), as they are looking at the whole child.

Nurturing a balance between intellectual/cognitive development and emotional/social development is very important. What does this mean? Why the new focus on "emotional IQ"? We live in a social world, where interacting with other people is inevitable unless we're hermits or live on a desert island, and then you wouldn't be reading this unless someone sent it to you in a bottle (sorry, I couldn't help myself). We aren't born with social skills such as knowing how to interact with others, to read people's emotions via body-language and facial expressions, we learn them. Similarly, we aren't born knowing what emotions are, what they mean, what to do with them, how to properly express them. These are all important things we have to learn, hopefully through our parents, family and siblings, otherwise by trial-and-error.

Parents have to be able to explain how they're feeling to their children so they're not misinterpreted. My favorite example of this is if a toddler (heaven forbid) starts to wander out onto a street between parked cars. The parent yells, runs to grab the child out of harms-way and appears livid. The child looks afraid and starts to cry, probably thinking that their parent is angry with them. After hearts stop pounding and cooler heads prevail, this is an opportunity to explain to the child that no one is angry, just terrified that something terrible could have happened. The child learns that their parent was desperately afraid that they could have been killed, not that it was an angry reaction...a perfect (if scary) learning opportunity. It also teaches children **empathy**, a very important interpersonal skill.

Empathy, or the ability to understand and respond appropriately to other people's feelings is the opposite of self-centeredness. Children need to learn that other people have feelings too and to be able to feel for them. Because children are born with an innate self-focus which they need in order to survive, they have to be taught that other people have feelings, which are no less important to them, and how to respond to them. Although our pets may not understand why we feel the way we do, have you ever noticed that a dog or cat will respond by trying to make you feel better when you feel sad? That's empathy...they seem to know how we feel and want to make us feel better. Sometimes there's nothing better than a puppy kiss or a cat purring on your lap to wipe away your tears!

When young children hit out in frustration, our first response may be anger, but I taught children and their parents what are "good touches", like hugs or tickles from people they know and trust and what are "bad touches", like a hit or a slap that makes people feel bad, hurt, or sad. This is, of course, irrespective of the "good touch/bad touch" programs children are taught about sexual abuse in schools. Hitting or slapping a child back only confuses them because it reinforces the behavior instead of stopping it. Talking about empathy, or how the other person feels, teaches them that other people have feelings and deserve to be treated with respect. It also teaches them to express their feelings in healthier ways and that they deserve respect, as well.

Children need to learn by example and they will mimic what they see, so if a parent only ever shows what appears to be anger when they're hurting or doesn't talk about their feelings (within limits), that's what they'll do as well. Then if the child does the same thing with their family or peers, they get blamed for doing what they've learned. How fair is that? Think of a child that gets frustrated by another child playing in the park. He or she jumps up and down and yells, maybe swears and is understandably ostracized, but what if that's what is seen at home by a parent in response to frustration? The old watch-word to "do as I say, not do as I do" seems hypocritical, doesn't it?

Play experiences before entering school are so important because siblings (unless they're twins) are not the same age or developmental level. Children need to learn to interact with each other with supervision and guidance in the beginning. If a child does not have the opportunity to play with others before he or she enters school, there may be some problems in getting along with others. Coaching is not just what team coaches do, coaching our children by gentle reminders, "rehearsing" or practicing social skills should begin at an early age. Children also watch us intently as we interact with friends and family, mimicking what they see by their behaviors. The admonishment about "little eyes and ears" is an important one to remember because if we don't watch what we say and do around our children, they may say or do what we don't want!

As much as I believe that parenting is about nurturance, the disciplinary part of it is equally important. A parent who only ever shows love and acceptance, without guiding a child when he or she has done wrong sets them up for failure. Clear expectations and structure, discipline and controls in place teach children self-discipline and self-control. They need to learn to get along, to take others into account, to compromise and negotiate. That doesn't mean that our rules are necessarily negotiable. We can explain them, but it doesn't mean we have to justify them when we enforce them. The difference in the school years is that children learn that other families may have different rules and expectations and then ours don't seem so absolute. Why do we set their bedtime or curfew earlier than others? Because it's what we believe is best for them. Sometimes our answers to "why" need to be just "because", end of story. I have sometimes seen parents so harassed by a child who won't accept what they're told that the parent gives in. What does that tell a child but to keep on questioning, keep undermining and you'll get what you want.

And then there's **chores**...something that every child should begin at an early age at a level that's age-appropriate. It teaches **responsibility**, **team-work** as a family and **self-respect**. Keeping their room clean is a given, picking up their toys around the house, helping with family pets, washing or drying dishes or loading or unloading the dishwasher, helping with yard-work, taking out the garbage, putting away their laundry and eventually doing their own laundry are not unreasonable expectations. A family chore list so that everyone does their share and rotates helps. We are not talking Cinderella here, children feel better about themselves when they can do things to take care of themselves. It never fails to amaze me when parents complain that their kids don't do anything around the house and hate being nagged, but they've never instituted a regular, enforced list of expectations.

Before we move on to school, I have to stop here for a moment and talk about the "whole child", not just the social, emotional and intellectual part. We know that there are so many other types of intelligence that often go unnoticed: creative, artistic, musical, athletic, and mechanical, among others. We nurture the social/emotional part by helping our children with play-dates and play-schools. Similarly, what stops us from nurturing their creative self with crafts and art projects, with baking, and sewing? Or their musical self with dancing to all kinds of music, or their athletic self with playing all sorts of sports with them? Or their mechanical side by having them help out in "fixing" things around the house, yard or garage? We don't have to "do it all", but having children involved in outside activities like sports teams, summer camps, art or music or drama classes is important to helping them find out what they enjoy, what they're good at and meet children with similar interests.

I was always saddened when I assessed a young person in trouble with the law for Court and as I went through their life history, so many had never done well in school or had any pro-social friends or had ever been on a sports team, taken any outside classes or camps. Many had never found anything they enjoyed or were good at, so they got themselves in trouble with similar bored, lonely peers. I can't help but wonder what would have happened differently in their lives if someone had taken an interest in them and in seeing what interested them...Sorry to preach, but it's a pattern I have seen over and over throughout the years and I want parents to be aware.

Chapter 11:

Our Family Tree: The School Years

School days begin our children's transition to the outside world even more. They learn to listen to other adults' and environments' rules and expectations. The "team approach" to working with our children's teachers and schools is an extremely important one. I have heard many times about my parents' day when if they got in trouble at school, they'd "get it" twice as much at home. Respecting others' rules and regulations is an important life-lesson. I can't tell you how many teachers nowadays bemoan the fact that so many parents don't back them up. The refrain of "it wasn't his/her fault" or "it was the other kid's fault" or "it was your (the teacher's) fault" is not a good message to give to a child. Don't get me wrong, there are personality differences and personality clashes between teachers and students and among students, and parents need to advocate for their children if they feel they have been wrongly accused, but where do children learn to respect others, their elders and authority figures?

I have a huge concern about the lack of respect for **others** in today's world. I believe that it begins at home and if children are not respected for their feelings, they will not learn to respect others. I remember speaking to a school-age child recently who told me that "respect is over-rated" and this shocked me. How we show and define respect may not be the same for all, but the fundamental right to our own feelings, to be treated and treat others fairly, to "do unto others" should be a given. When I was growing up, "respecting your elders" was an obligation/expectation, however they acted towards us. Today, I really believe that respect should be mutual...if we are treated with respect and decency, we should give it back.

Teaching our children to respect **themselves** is extremely important. What does that mean? Taking care of their hygiene and appearance is crucial to show the world that they care about themselves. (I am sorry, but it is very hard to take a child or teenager seriously who wears their pants so baggy that they're around their ankles or shows off more cleavage or midriff than you'd see at the beach.) Learning to express themselves in age-appropriate ways, not by yelling and throwing a tantrum, shows others that they deserve to be listened to. Otherwise, they'll be teased or ignored, feeling even worse about themselves.

With self-respect comes self-coaching. Remember that inner voice I was talking about a few chapters back? This is where it comes in. Children need to learn to recognize when they have done well and feel good about it. Similarly, they need to be able to explain to themselves and understand how they could have done better (remember the Little Engine That Could?) without destroying their self-confidence. We aren't always going to be around our children in performance or social situations, so we have to teach them to praise themselves within reason ("give yourself a pat on the back"), to admonish themselves when they should, and coach themselves to do better.

Meeting the teachers for parent-teacher interviews with our children lets them see that we're on the "same page", that we're working together to help them. We show them that how they feel and what they say is important, but it is within the larger context of how they relate to others. The world is not all about them and they have to learn to get along, to work together and listen while being listened to at the same time. It shows mutual respect, trying to understand the full picture of their lives with others.

Elementary school, with the nurturance and child-focus of classroom teachers who get to know our children, their personalities and capabilities, working together with them individually graduates to junior high school. What a potential mess! We've got hormonal, pre-pubertal pre-teens in a new setting with new kids, and more teachers in individual subjects. The poor kids have to learn to deal with new people, new expectations, and feelings they've never even felt before. The focus begins to shift away from parents and home more to their peers, who become their new "family". So many kids have told me that they can talk to their friends much more easily than to their parents and parents begin to feel that they don't know these new creatures who return home from school or being with their friends to their rooms, the television, their cell phones and their computers. ("What do you mean I'm grounded...I can't survive without my laptop, my cell phone, and my friends!") Rather than becoming less important, I feel that the family becomes even **more** important with family dinners, family outings, and mom-and-dad "chats". We desperately need to "keep-in-touch" with our pre-teens, to know their friends and their friends' parents, their teachers, and their coaches, among others.

The whole opposite-sex thing becomes a big issue in junior high. Even if kids in elementary school say that they have "boy/girl-friends", usually it's nothing serious. I have to stop here and note that children are having sex earlier and earlier all the time. It is sadly not unusual for children to try having sex at 12 or 13 or even earlier. Please don't shoot the messenger as I am as upset about it as anyone. Despite better sex education, the media presents sexuality in dressing style and behavior as the way to be and parents buy the clothes, the make-up, and let kids watch the shows. Don't get me going on this topic, because it could go on for days...nevertheless, kids want to start "going out" around mid-junior high school. I know I must sound old-fashioned (and I am in many ways), but they don't seem to "date" anymore. They "hang-out" together "24/7", seeing each other at school, going to each other's houses, on the phone with each other every night or on social media...what happened to the excitement of having your daughter's date bus it over on a Friday or Saturday night and chat with him anxiously as she gets ready? It seems to have gone the way of the dinosaur and when I talk to kids about it, their eyes glaze over, uncomprehending. Come on, this is not Victorian-era-type stuff and I'm not that old!

Curfew becomes more of an issue as kids try to test the waters and see how late they can stay out. If their friends' parents let them stay out later or not come home at night, how come they can't? My stock phrase is that it's because I care about them and it's easy to be a parent when you don't have rules. Parents who care show that they do because it takes effort and disagreements, more as the kids become teens. Remember, they see us as stupider when they become teens. Suddenly we "don't understand" anymore, unlike their parents as preschoolers, who knew everything. Take heart, stick-to-your-beliefs and hold on for the ride, because high school is coming!

Luckily, when kids get to high school as opposed to junior high, we don't have the hormonal shift, but they are still fully hormonal. They become even more educationally independent and self-reliant as there are different teachers for every subject and they become overwhelmed because the teachers don't talk when it comes to assigning homework. They could have homework in every subject one night and we have to make sure to teach them time-management, not to procrastinate and to "prioritize". And that's if they're going to school...some kids refuse outright, saying they don't legally have to as of age 16 here in Canada. Many begin by starting to skip classes with like-minded peers. Even if they had the intention of going to class, if a friend is going to skip, it makes it easier. Even in this day and age, with the greater competition for jobs, a more highly educated job-market, increased specialization in the work-force, you're sometimes preaching to deaf ears because you're talking rationally and they're not thinking rationally.

What if a youth refuses to go to school? Insist that they have to pay rent if they're not in school and then they have to get a job. (You can even tally up the rent money and give it to them when they move out, which I've seen some savvy parents do over the years.) Then, they'll get to see the real world and realize that they don't want to work at "fast-food" forever. I have seen a growing trend with young people moving into their friends' houses when the going-gets-tough at home and this is very distressing, as it disempowers parents from doing what they think is right. I personally think it's wrong to take in another parent's child (unless of course there's abuse happening and then you get in the proper authorities), because they have a right to parent their child and no one has a right to judge them. More on parents and their teens in a couple of chapters...

When the kids have successfully negotiated their way into adulthood, hopefully having finished school and on their way to a career or higher education, feel proud! They've made it and you've helped them get there...a few more wrinkles and grey hairs, but it was worth it! You couldn't be their friend before, because they weren't ready for it, but now you can work towards a more balanced relationship since there is no more need for a power dynamic. You can both enjoy the fruits of the hard work it took to grow up and become a parent!

Chapter 12:

Our Children, Our Teachers

What do we learn from being parents? From the very beginning, we learn so much...during pregnancy, to take care of ourselves because it's taking care of them. Many people take out life insurance when their children are born, realizing their own mortality and the responsibility they have to the new life they've brought into this world. As infants, we learn to try and interpret their needs by their cries...do they need a cuddle, a meal, a diaper-change? Are they in pain? Just ask a bleary-eyed parent with a colicky baby...what are they telling you? How do you help them? How do you make them stop crying? Everyone has a solution: take them for a drive, run the vacuum cleaner, put them safely on the dryer, hold them close and rock them. What about a child born prematurely? How do you bond with an infant in an incubator, wanting to hold them close and rock them, feed them, cuddle them? Their mere existence has taught us to love unselfishly and unconditionally, to give our love without expecting anything else in return. That's lesson #1.

Hearing a baby cry inconsolably, and trying everything we can to somehow meet whatever need they're trying to communicate teaches us: patience. So does responding to "no's" from a toddler over and over again. So does answering countless questions we've never even asked ourselves about the world around us. So does children making the same mistakes over and over despite what we keep telling them. So does sibling rivalry, tattle-telling, defiance, talking-back, and fibbing, among many others. Being a parent tests our patience beyond any bounds we could ever imagine and shows our children how to deal with frustration.

We learn better emotional skills, ourselves, as we model how to express our feelings in healthier ways because that's how our children learn, by our example. Our communication skills improve as we have to explain the reasons why we do what we do, how we feel, what we want and what we need. We learn better team approaches out of necessity, with our spouses and family, as well as our children. Delegating tasks and chores is a part of this, teaching responsibility and self-respect. Trust for your spouse should also improve and grow, as you work together as parents.

Being a parent, with all of its challenges and dedication of time should also teach a person that their own individual needs and their couple needs are important. It's easy to take yourself for granted because between making lunches for school the next day, doing laundry, cooking meals, cleaning the house, getting kids bathed before bedtime, recycling, working, getting groceries, paying bills, getting kids to and from school and to all their activities, who else can make time for you? This is so important, because when a person's needs go unmet, they can become unhappy, resentful and bitter.

Fitting in couple time, too, is a challenge but so very important. A couple can grow together as parents, working together for the children, building greater trust and respect for each other, communicating better and cherishing their (stolen moments) time together when the kids are in bed or at activities or out on "dates".

Parenting teaches us to be more honest with ourselves because we have to be honest with our children. If we lie to them, how do we expect them to be honest with us? We may not always like what we find out about ourselves as we grow into parenthood. Maybe we have too much of a temper, maybe we're too impatient, maybe too self-involved, maybe too passive or too selfless, but we can always grow and mature throughout our whole lives.

Parenthood can make us more objective about our own childhoods, rethinking and not accepting all of what our parents did with us. That's a good thing, because unquestioning acceptance without critical awareness makes people repeat old habits, some of which may not be good ones. It can also improve the relationships with our own parents, asking their advice about the things they warned us about ("just remember this when you have your own kids" or "I hope you have a kid just like you").

Everything we teach our children, from empathy to social skills, from assertiveness to time-management, from responsibility to self-respect, from conflict-management to learning to manage their allowance money makes us grow. All of this from when they were just a "twinkle in our eye", our world becomes a different and better place. Can you tell I love being a mother? They have taught me so much.

Chapter 13:

Parents and Teens: Who is Really Having an Identity Crisis?

Now that we've got the glow from seeing how much we've learned from being a parent, let's look at our own life-circumstances by the time our kids are teens. When I point out what I'm going to explain to you to teenagers, they're very surprised but thoughtful, because it explains a lot. What are the biggest peeves that parents have about their teenagers? Their health, their relationships, their education and their future careers top the list.

As far as their health is concerned, that includes getting enough sleep, eating right, not drinking and doing drugs, as well as safe sex. Why? Because when our kids become teenagers, we're already on the downswing or have plateaued, getting some grey hair and wrinkles, overtired, and trying to keep our younger physiques. We want them to take care of their health by eating right (not just junk food and fast food), getting some exercise, sleeping enough (getting a teenager to bed and getting them up in the morning can be a nightmare), not poisoning themselves with drugs or alcohol or getting a communicable disease.

Diet, sleep and exercise are self-explanatory, but let's look at the pressures to drink and do drugs in today's day and age. New alcoholic products that taste and look like pop or "Kool-Aid" come out every day. When I walk my dog late at night, I notice "cooler" bottles out on the field or near the bushes nearby after the weekend. I know I am making an assumption, but why would adults be drinking outside late at night, away from watching eyes? It's so easy for kids nowadays to get someone 18 or older to "boot" alcohol for them and it's at almost every party, as my daughter attests. To her credit, she would ask me to pick her up from parties that are too alcohol- or drug-laden because she thought it's a stupid waste of time. More and more designer drugs come out all the time. Drugs are laced with worse drugs and every high school has its share of "stoners" and "dealers", even some junior high schools! My daughter has told me that she used to get asked every day if she wanted to "get high". Talk about pressure! Of course we're concerned about our kids and drugs!

Then, there's sex...not a new concept, but there are new and virulent, lethal STDs out there and kids are having sex sooner. I can't tell you the number of teenagers nowadays who are already burdened with herpes for life from one sexual encounter. And it goes on and on...of course we're concerned! The world is a scarier place than when we grew up, more dangerous, potentially lethal, right in our own backyard. But they don't want to learn from our mistakes, they have to make their own...

As for our kids' relationships, at our age our marriages have either plateaued or dissolved and we want them to choose the **right one**, not that the first will be forever. The "24/7" thing, at the expense of school, other friends and family can be overwhelming. When they put so much energy, so much hope and so many dreams, "all their eggs in one basket", instead of dating to find out want they want, what they don't want, it can be pretty scary. But don't try and pry them apart! Have you not read "Romeo and Juliet"? The more you pull them apart, the tighter they become, so you sit by helplessly waiting for their heart to break, hoping it happens but it won't hurt too much. Hopefully, they'll eventually find the "right one" and we can celebrate together (without saying "I told you so" out loud).

How about school? We know how important it is in this day and age. We are firmly invested in our jobs/careers, whether we like them or not. We have bills to pay, seniority of years in towards retirement. We may have our regrets about "what might have been" if we had taken a different road in education or career path and now we see our teens with all doors open wide to them. Do they realize how important it is to make sure their bases are covered, ensure that they're taking the right courses and getting the best marks they can? With so many kids wanting to get higher education, there are more people for fewer spaces and grade expectations are higher. It's not just grade 12 marks they look for now, but also grade 11 marks, to ensure that a student has "staying power" or dedication to their education. Of course we're concerned about their education because it's their future, but do they see it?

As I explained these scenarios to teens, graphically showing how they're on the way upwards into their own futures and their parents are either stuck or on their way downwards in these areas, they understand that it's not coming from nowhere, that their parents are not trying to control them but speaking from their own experience. It makes a huge difference as they see the "big picture". They get so caught up in the power dynamic that they miss the rational reasons from their parents' experience that drives their concerns. You'd be surprised at the "light bulbs going off" and the empathy and understanding that helps reconnect them back to their parents.

As I kept explaining to kids and teens, if they show self-control and self-discipline, they don't have to be controlled or disciplined or nagged. Parents and teens can work together, and when it works, it's great!

Chapter 14:
Don't Change Me, Just Let Me Grow!

Life is about growth and change. From birth to death we continue to become who we are meant to be. Development doesn't stop when we become adults. I remember being a child and then a teenager, excited to reach a place in my life when I had **become**, but what? I saw people in their twenties as having gotten there, satisfied with their lives and then when I got there, I realized: not yet. So, I looked at people in their thirties and thought they must have it figured out, but when I got there, I saw that they were still looking. I realized that there was no magical age when you become who you are meant to be. We are all a work in progress, right up until we are no longer on this earth, but some people have more or less happiness along the way. It's very true that it is not the destination that makes us happy, it's the road that takes us there.

I've worked with many people along my way who were dealing with end-of-life issues: agonizing about whether they did okay, if they could have done better, all the "what-ifs". One of the dearest, sweetest older people agonized about whether she should have been more affectionate with her spouse, whether they should have held hands more. I asked her what was stopping her now. When we met for the last time, with a twinkle in her eye and a gentle smile on her face, she told me that they always held hands now when they went out. Life is about no regrets, no what-ifs, or you'll never know. She taught me a lot, dear sweet lady: that we're never too old to learn and grow if it's important enough to us.

When people are told that they have to change or else, it sounds like an ultimatum. Ultimatums make people feel resentful. It's as simple as that. For instance, when I worked with people who came to see me in order to quit smoking, my first question to them was: why do you want to quit? If they say it's because they're being pressured by their family, I wouldn't even begin. The reason is that they need to do it because **they** want to quit. If they quit because others want them to, it won't work, or maybe only for a short time. Their own reason to maintain the habit is too strong and there's a great temptation to cheat, which sets them up for failure.

Changing for someone else because they tell you to is for their needs, or it seems to be. It tells a person that he or she could be "better" somehow, that what they are doing is not good enough. Telling a person that you worry about them, that what they are doing hurts them or you is a different matter. It's sharing how you feel, what you need. It invites **growth**, potentially learning a new way to do things. They may figure out a better way, but they have to decide for themselves. It's a fine line.

People do grow and learn throughout their lives. Some have to learn the hard way: making mistakes, sometimes over and over again. We know this as parents because we'd love nothing better than for our offspring to learn from **our** mistakes, so that they don't have to endure failure or pain. Many times, they may listen but they still try and do things their own way just like we did. It's not just parents or adults that kids don't learn from, many times I hear the same refrain from younger siblings to their older brothers or sisters: "Let me make my own mistakes!" It's not always so black and white though, as they may listen when it comes to schoolwork but not when given advice regarding relationships.

Maybe that is the way life is meant to be sometimes: growing through pain. As we grow physically, we experience "growing pains". Perhaps the emotional marker of hurt or pain is enough to teach us to try things a different way. If it hurt us by not studying (and failing a test or course) or not working hard enough (and getting a warning or fired from a job) or not listening to our significant other (and getting into an argument or losing the relationship), how long would it take us to change? Hopefully not too long, but sometimes people don't see the patterns of failure or unhappiness in their lives. It depends upon what they attribute their consequences to, or how they explain outcomes.

The reasons we give ourselves for success or failure are called **attributions**. We also make attributions about why we see others succeed or fail. People have different attributional styles based on past experience, personality type and what they have been taught, among other factors. Depending upon how they explain their experiences, it either motivates them or reduces their motivation to succeed. It may even lead to feelings of helplessness and depression.

If a person succeeds at something and they explain their success as due to their ability ("I'm good at this"), they feel good about themselves. If they explain a success as due to their effort ("I tried/studied hard"), they also feel good about themselves. Both these explanations are internal (due to them), but the effort is also something that they can control. If they explain a success as due to the task being easy or that they had good luck, neither is within their control. They wouldn't feel as good about themselves because it had less to do with them. Internalized success experiences make people feel good, it's as simple as that.

Now let's look at failure experiences. No one feels good about failing, but sometimes we can learn from it to change the outcome to a success experience the next time. If a person fails at a task, whether it's at school or work or in a relationship, it's in how they explain it that they can potentially learn. If they think it's due to bad luck, there's nothing they can do about it, as it's unpredictable and out of their control. If they think it's due to someone else and not themselves, again it's out of their control. Both of these explanations would make them feel bad because there's nothing they can do about it. If they explain a failure as due to lack of effort, they could change the outcome next time by trying harder. It's within their control.

There are more resilient attributional styles that help preserve a person's self-esteem and motivation. Attributing success to a reason that is internal (ability or personality) and controllable (effort) allows them to feel that they can be successful again. Attributing failure to a reason that is controllable (lack of effort) also gives them something to work towards by working harder next time. A more depressive, or "glass half empty" view of the world causes a person to explain their successes as due to good luck (uncontrollable) or an easy task (external and unpredictable). Similarly, an individual who views the world this way would explain failures as due to bad luck (uncontrollable) or their personality or ability (internal, unchangeable). It is easy to see how these individuals would give up in the face of failure: if there's nothing they can do to change it or it's out of their control, why keep on trying?

Most people want to feel in control over their lives, at least to some extent. There are some things that we can't control, however and it's important to be able to make that distinction. If someone feels that his or her life is controlled by others, this can lead to frustration and resentment. Not being able to be or express oneself can be very crippling. Feeling that one has no impact on what happens in life, that bad luck or hostile people or bad situations just keep happening leaves very little room for hope or change. How can a person want to grow if they feel that others will just continue to ignore them or their efforts?

Feeling in control over our lives, realistically so, gives us a sense of empowerment, of purpose and self-direction. If we feel that others are stunting our growth or trying to make us become what we're not, this can lead to several outcomes. It can result in anger and resentment, expressed negatively towards others or to hopelessness and dejection that can be internalized and expressed negatively towards ourselves.

Whether or not we welcome it, life is about change: time passes, we age, our children grow up, our loved ones die. These we have to accept and people do to varying degrees. Have you noticed people in your everyday lives who age gracefully, let the "laugh lines" show, and let their hair grow grey if they want to? They seem to accept the aging process as part of life, not running to have every wrinkle "botoxed", every grey hair dyed, every curve "liposuctioned". They actually seem to have more energy to give to life than others who exhaust themselves seeking the fountain of youth in creams and surgeries. I am forever amazed at the age-spread at my gym where I work out, with many more of us "oldsters" working from the inside-out. I firmly believe that mental/emotional health works hand-in-hand with physical health, both in terms of exercise and nutrition. There was a reason our parents sent us out during those cold winters to toboggan and skate, returning home rosy-cheeked to warm up with hot chocolate, rather than sit at home and vegetate by a video-game or computer.

We know that our children are going to grow up and become independent, to move away and have their own lives. That's what we work so hard to prepare them for: the lives we want them to succeed and be happy in. This is good change; growth for them and a chance at growth for us as individuals, as grandparents and in-laws. There is fear that comes with this change, however, as we worry about how they will survive, wanting to protect them from the world we have no control over. All we can do is give them all of the tools we know, the self-confidence, self-discipline, self-control, self-respect and self-love that makes them know they're worthwhile. The personal fears of empty-nesters include looking across the kitchen table at their spouse one day and realizing that all they have in common is that they're "mom" or "dad", and haven't kept up with growing as a couple or as individuals. More about this later.

The inevitability of death in our lives increases as each generation passes on. Our safety cushion becomes thinner as we see grandparents (or great-grandparents if you're lucky), then our parents' generation start to thin out. It's a scary realization of our own mortality and the loss of our past, the shared experiences and memories that we are left to carry on to further generations. I will never forget the loss of my maternal grandfather, the sweetest, most gentle man I have ever met. I spent countless hours in my childhood by his side, listening to stories of the "old country", of his and my grandmother's life there that I have passed onto my own children. They are enchanted by them and will hopefully share them with their own children. My brother, eight years younger than me, was not as fortunate to have shared the stories in my grandfather's own voice. I remember getting the idea of recording them in his own words, but he sadly passed just as I was preparing to make tapes of them. The loss of his gentle voice, his accent and patient repetition of the same stories over and over again was a great one for me. Yet, his past lives on in me, in my memories of his memories, just as I have passed it on to my own next generation.

Death, the final passage in our own and our loved one's lives is something that we cannot change. We can spend our lives pretending that it won't happen, not preparing ourselves for the loss, the void it leaves in our lives. If we don't accept it, however, how can we ever appreciate the time together? I love the admonition to say every goodbye as if it was our last, to always let people know how much we love them so there are no regrets. I can't tell you the countless times I've had to help people through their grief, agonizing over whether their loved one knew how much they loved them. Every night, even after a disagreement, I have kissed and hugged my children, told them I loved them, wishing for them to fall asleep feeling loved. It's the same for phone calls or visits to elderly relatives: you never know when a hug or a kiss or an "I love you" may be for the last time.

Fear of our own deaths makes some people afraid to live. They stop themselves from experiencing life to its fullest: the smells, the colors, the tastes, the feelings, the relationships, the experiences and challenges. Again, we return to the saying: "no regrets". How many times have people chased themselves away from life experiences out of fear and regretted it later? How many relationships could have been the "right one", the "soul mate" who was avoided out of fear of rejection? They'll never know. Life is about taking chances, calculated risks and many times, people are pleasantly surprised when they try something "out of character".

Something that I am struck by when I speak to older people about their lives, which I love to do because they have so much to tell, so much wisdom to share, is how they look back on what they have done. While they take stock of their lives, what they have accomplished and created in their families, many still think of the "road less traveled", other paths they might have taken, what "might have been". With time running short, many make peace with knowing that they won't be able to do all that they wanted to do in one lifetime. It's inevitable, yet at the other end of it, youth has all the optimism that they have all the time in the world. Reality sets in with age.

In our day and age, is the focus on personal growth a luxury that previous generations didn't have the time to even think about? Did they have time to wonder if they were happy, with working from dawn to dusk in order to survive? Our world changes now at such a rapid pace that we have to keep up with it or fall to the wayside like the dinosaurs. I was an avowed computer illiterate right up until the end of my Master's degree, dutifully typing and editing and re-editing the drafts of my thesis. I had no problem with doing my statistics on the main-frame (using computer cards, so that I had a hard-copy), but the fluidity of a computer screen to write on baffled and terrified me. Would it lose what I had written? Inevitably, it did at times because I forgot to save what I had written every so often. It sure made editing the drafts of my dissertation a thousand times easier. Eventually, I adapted as my mother-in-law surpassed me at computer skills and egged me on. She really did believe that when we stop learning, we will die and embodied this right up until the end.

Growth is adaptation to change. Those who don't adapt are less likely to succeed and survive, according to Darwin. Life is about survival of the fittest, and since we don't have generations to adapt our bodies to all of the change that is happening around us, we have to adapt our minds and learn in order to cope. Coping is about growing into change. Change can be in the form of new technology, new relationships (such as in the birth of children or a marriage), a new job, a change in financial circumstances, a new school, in one's health, or in the loss of a relationship (through divorce or death), among others. We have to grow into dealing with these new things in our lives, learning as we go along if it is new to us. Just because someone has coped with a change in their lives before doesn't mean that the same strategies will work again successfully. This is where adaptability comes into play, the ability to apply new strategies to survive and succeed. Whereas the species that Darwin studied had to take generations to mutate into surviving in their environments, we don't have just our bodies to compensate. We have our minds and ingenuity, our heart and our feelings to work together in order to survive and live.

We are experienced at the skills it takes to grow and survive. We do it naturally, some more easily than others. Being told to change when we feel that we are doing fine sometimes feels like an affront. If a person likes the way they are and is happy with themselves, they may not see a reason to change. Yet a new relationship is something else to adjust to, to adapt to. If you are happy within yourself with how you are, and feel that it is more worthwhile to stay that way, you may take the risk of losing a relationship. If it means losing yourself, the very core of your being to be acceptable to someone else, it may cost too much to remain in a relationship. Some minor changes to "fine-tune" a relationship may be worth it, however, in order to make someone else happy. Some people are more amenable to changing for others, but there is a fine line between pleasing others and being pleased with yourself. There are some that lose themselves in relationships, being so anxious to be accepted and acceptable.

It all comes down to a balance between the need to be yourself or who you consider yourself to be and the need to be part of a relationship. Some people will not compromise who they are to fit with someone else. Others feel a greater need to be with someone else and are willing to change themselves for that person. The balancing trick is in meeting your own needs, while at the same time meeting others'.

Chapter 15:

What is missing from My Life? What am I Really Looking For?

So you have a career, a spouse, a family and everything and everyone seems to be doing fine. The bills are paid, your job is okay and you like the people there, you and your spouse get along fine most of the time, the kids are happy and healthy, doing alright in school and with their friends. How come you're not happy? Welcome to a larger group out there of disenchanted people who can empathize more than you even realize.

Something is missing. Even though people have more, do more and know more than ever before, they're not as happy as they want to be. Why? Is ignorance truly bliss? Does having more and having the money to do more make them any happier? Is the fact that the world is smaller than ever before, little is unattainable and people theoretically have more time to enjoy it helping? Or is knowing more of what others have through the magazines about the stars and the wealthy too much to aspire to? From the tabloids, even the "have's" aren't happy, look at the length of their marriages!

What are people so busy looking for and not finding? Many are doing mid-career changes, getting further or different training, finding their jobs or careers are unfulfilling. Many are leaving "comfortable" marriages because they're "not in love" anymore or may have found someone else. These are huge external life-changes that impact on so many people: families, spouses, children, employees and the workplace. Do these external changes make them happier or should they be looking inside themselves?

Earlier on, I brought up the issue of people having "passions": things/activities/pets that make them feel good. The other day, I watched a television show about the rescue by the SPCA of abandoned pets in the New Orleans area after Hurricane Katrina. The residents had been ordered to leave their pets when they were rescued and seeing the looks on their faces when they reunited with them showed pure joy. One elderly retired gentleman had only one living being left that he loved: his cat and he had tried to brave every restriction and weather condition to get her back. He did, and when he returned to his house, all he took with him was the cat and her toys and food. He felt complete with her unconditional love.

Searching inside ourselves, there are buried wants, needs and desires that we've either ignored or never taken the time to listen to. I'm not saying that people can't have obsessions with pastimes, sports or activities, and that they can potentially take precedence over life (just talk to a "golf-"or "baseball-widow"). I'm just asking you to ask yourself: what would fulfill you? Greater intimacy in your marriage, becoming each other's best friends (hopefully again)? More closeness with your children, spending more time with them and getting to know them? Reconnection with your extended family or long-lost relatives? Reuniting with old school-chums? Getting a chance to try out the "what-if's"? There are so many movies about old sportsters trying out for teams they never thought they could, following their dreams. The themes really "hit close to home" for many of us.

What do you dream about? What have you hardly dared to dream about because it would hurt so much when you wake up to reality? What does it cost to dream, anything? I loved doing future-hypnosis with people because they could envision themselves doing what they've only ever dreamed of. Sometimes, they told me that it felt so good, they had to "go for it" (within reason, of course)...like owning their own business or finding the love-of-their-life.

With more time on our hands than ever before due to automation, household gadgets, ready-made foods, cars to get us places faster, malls in almost every suburb and faster forms of communication like the internet, cell-phones and fax machines, we should have more time for family, our spouses and ourselves. What do so many people fill up their spare time with...television, the endless mind-numbing, passive "window-to-the-world".

What do many children do after school now, other than playing video-games or talking to each other on the computer? They watch television. Don't get me wrong, I loved Saturday morning cartoons or Sunday-night's "Wide World of Disney", "Sesame Street" with my little brother after school, or "Gilligan's Island", "Bewitched" and "I Dream of Jeannie", but what else did we do after school? We read Nancy Drew or Hardy Boys mysteries, read Archie comics and did puzzles or Spirograph on our own. We played outside with friends...games like tag, hide-and-seek, Red Robin, Mother May I, Red-Light Green-Light, handball against the garage wall, basketball, and dodge-ball, among others. We went to each other's houses to play board games or dress-up or Barbie's or GI Joe's or Lego or made pretend houses out of boxes. We went tobogganing or skating in winter, made snow-forts and had snow-ball fights. We didn't decide whose house to go to by who had the better video-games. We made our fun and used our **imaginations**. I am so worried that we are raising a generation of children whose only imagination is what they see in movies, on computers or video-games.

There certainly are intelligent choices on television such as the nature channels, Public Broadcasting, and history channels, among others. There are potential learning opportunities from television, but so much more time is spent on the sitcoms, the soap operas (late-night and day-time), and the series that occupy our mental time to escape this world. In mentally running away from this world, we are not taking the time to listen to ourselves, what we are thinking, what we are feeling, what we want and what we need. We fill up our minds with what the screen shows us, pretending for a while that we're not really here in our lives. The commercial breaks bring us back to reality and people run for the bathroom or a snack or drink, to return in time to take them back to that other world, transfixed. The same goes for the movies...how much is spent on making them and how much do they make, as people spend more and more money going to the theatres to drift away for a little while?

There used to be a television in the living room. Now they're in bedrooms and children's bedrooms. People fall asleep watching TV, trying to catch the last bit of the news or late-night talk-shows. They're tired when they wake up, wishing they'd gone to sleep earlier. Children watch videos or TV in their rooms and parents argue with them about sleep times because their favorite show is on. People have TVs in their kitchens so that meal-time can be watching together. Where's the family sharing time? Even TVs in the bathroom...what happened to that time for contemplation? We bombard ourselves with outside stimulation, outside information and in the process, have lost touch with ourselves, our own thoughts, and our own "family news". While television has brought the world together in a global sharing of information, we have let it make us farther apart in our relationships and from ourselves. And then there are the arguments over remote-controls and changing radio stations in the car...what have we come to?

I really believe that if more time was spent in our **own** reality, not just existing or surviving in it but really **living** in it, we'd work much harder to make it better. Don't get me wrong, I watch some television to occupy my mind sometimes. Do I know when specific shows are on? No. Do I plan my life around catching the next installment of a series? No. Do I run to be the one of the first to see a new movie? No. I'll wait to catch it on video in my own time. Why? Because I want to live my own life with all its ups and downs, not someone else's and that's my choice.

If I look back historically at when the world began to change, from families eating together at the dinner table to "TV tables" grouped around the television, to children running home from school to catch the latest sitcom before doing their homework, to couples having "quality time together" watching a movie on television or in the theatre, that's where I believe we lost touch with ourselves and each other. Who cares how an actress does her hair on a television show? Millions of women who spend millions of dollars trying to look like her. Who cares what tennis, golf equipment or running shoes a famous athlete uses? Millions of people who run out to buy the same product. When did we become so superficial? Does it make us any happier? What happened to working on ourselves from the inside out?

Thinking and feeling are free! We can do them anytime! Talking with our family, our children, and our friends is free! We don't necessarily need to plan it, schedule it, buy a phone-card or "log-on" to do it. They're out there waiting! People put such a distance between themselves and who they care about, when all they need to do is take the time. They maintain a distance from themselves by keeping pre-occupied so they don't have to think. The thinking is done for them by what they watch on television or their feelings are left buried while they "feel" for people they see in movies and on television. The lives of the "rich and famous" become their envy to aspire to, not recognizing or appreciating what they have right at home.

Television is "meta-life", watching other people or characters live their lives. How about living your own life, the life that you want? Who cares what was worn at the Oscars or who won a music award? How about what your child wore at a school play or what's "your song" from when you first met? These are the **real memories** about **real life**, not someone else's reality.

Take time to replay your own internal videos of life before...what made you happy? What did you enjoy, look forward to, and get excited about? What made you sad, what did you dread? Children love to hear stories of our childhood, our past lives, when Mom and Dad met, their babyhood, and the funny anecdotes. These are the family memories to share, of generations past and present. World history has been carried on through stories and song...is our own family history any less important?

No one knows you or should know you better than you. No one can tell you how to feel or what would make you feel happier, it's up to you to. Just take the time to listen to yourself, uninterrupted, your own internal dialogue of feelings, memories, wants and needs. It's there waiting for you, anytime you choose to listen.

Chapter 16:

Life is about Balance

"Everything in moderation" is a familiar refrain. We can eat what we want (a "balanced diet") if we exercise to work it off. We can take as long as we give. We can work hard, as long as we get enough rest. We can play as long as we work ("all work and no play..."). The same goes for meeting our own needs: we can keep giving of ourselves as long as we fill ourselves up, otherwise the unselfishness becomes an imbalance that ends in resentment and unhappiness. The same goes for family and couple needs: giving of our time, our energy, our emotion sustains them, but we need to get something back. Again, the imbalance of giving and giving and not receiving or taking and not giving back creates unhappiness.

We need balance, or an equilibrium within ourselves and within our relationships. Self-denial is unhealthy, denial of ourselves for our partners and our families demonstrates a lack of self-respect. People can take advantage of it, for example do you know someone who just can't say no? That person gets taken advantage of constantly, eventually feels taken for granted and resentful over time but a pattern has been set up that others respond to because they know that person will always agree to help. I return to the wonderful ability, which can be learned, to be **assertive**: saying how you feel, what you want and what you need. No one can do it for you, only you know for yourself.

There are certainly times in relationships when someone needs more than they can give, as in the saying "in sickness and in health". People expect that and should be prepared to show that they care, but it has to be reciprocated at some point. It's not an obligation, but it should be an expectation that goes unsaid. Appreciation and recognition go a long way to making a person feel worthwhile, so does reciprocation.

Do you know someone who always remembers birthdays and anniversaries, giving you a call when you think everyone forgot? How great does that make your day?! To be remembered, without reminders is a gift in itself. How does that person feel if people forget their special day? To know that we're in someone else's thoughts makes us feel special. I can't tell you how many times, as my day progresses, I think of someone I worked with in the past and sure enough, I get a call from them soon after. It's uncanny really, because I know that even if I haven't heard from them in a long time, they'll be calling me. It's happened so many times over the years and I can't explain it. All I know is that thinking of others makes them thoughtful of you. Thinking of and considering yourself makes you mindful of your own feelings and needs.

It's such a simple equation, really...what goes out has to be balanced by what goes in and vice-versa. When I spoke to people about losing weight, for instance, they were very concerned about what they ate and the quantities, but food is just our human version of gasoline. What's pumped in is either worked off or stored as fat. Exercise to work off any excessive fuel is crucial to ensure that the system remains in balance. Starvation or eating one meal a day makes the body think it is being starved and it stores food as fat, so eating in moderation and exercising is the way to keep things in balance.

Let's take this analogy to relationships...filling up too much from what your partner gives creates an imbalance in them if you don't give back. Giving of yourself continually without being "filled up" by those who love you empties a person's reserves. That feeling of emptiness, sadness, lack of fulfilment has to be replenished...either by yourself or others. Otherwise, that "hole", that empty well inside gets so low that there's little energy to give to yourself, never mind others.

So how to do this, to ensure that reserves don't get too low? Being reactive, after-the-fact is sometimes almost too late. I've worked with too many people through the years who have let themselves get so low that it's like an internal switch has gone off so that they can't feel their emotions, good or bad. Needless to say, that's not good. It's always better to be pro-active, catching those emotions before they get too low. It's harder to restart the "emotions switch" after you hit "empty" than it is to refuel when you feel yourself getting low.

More practically, what makes you feel good, what fills you up? What hurts you or makes you feel bad? The old refrain returns to my mind: "Doctor, doctor, it hurts when I do this...then don't do that!" If you know that something hurts, why would you keep doing it? If you know that something makes you feel good or at least better, as long as it's not hurting yourself or anyone else, why not just do it? It's just like in relationships: if it hurts more than it feels good, try to change it but if you can't, then you have a decision to make. Why would you stay in something that ultimately makes you feel worse?

It's one thing to recognize what it is that you want or need from someone. That's a great first step...but if they don't know what you're feeling and what you need or want, how can they know what you need? No one is a mind-reader and we can't assume that "they should know". That's where we come back to communication...the give-and-take of expressing yourself and listening to yourself and others.

There are many ways to "fill up", some healthy and some not-so-healthy. That's where "comfort foods" come in and "shopping therapy", the quick-fix to feel better in the short-run. The extra pounds and high charge-card bills are a reminder that they are not a long-term solution but may actually contribute to more problems.

In an earlier chapter when I talked about the elements of a healthy relationship, I mentioned how differently people express and receive love, and how sometimes there is an imbalance in how it is expressed relative to how their partner may want to receive it. Telling someone you love them may be what they want to hear, but if showing them in little gestures, time together or small gifts is what they want, it's not sufficient. In a similar vein, how do you show yourself that you're worthwhile? If working out at the gym makes you feel better about your body and yourself, why not do it? If taking your dog for a walk makes you and him or her feel good, why not do it? If taking time to read a book you've been saving would feel good, why not do it?

Yes, time is often short, but why not schedule in some "stolen moments" for yourself, just like the "stolen moments" for you and your spouse? Are you not important? If everyone else is more important than you make yourself, who is there to insist you do it for yourself? If you don't appreciate you, who is going to? If you don't take care of yourself, who is going to? People keep putting things off until "later", like couples who wait to do something together (like travel) when they're retired and then unfortunately one of them dies soon after. Was waiting worth it?

There are so many "what-if's" we all have about our lives, the "should've dones" and then time passes us by. Then we're that much older, that much wiser, that much more tired. If you can do something that you enjoy now, what is stopping you? Why not make it a priority, just like time-management of daily tasks...schedule in some "me" time, even 15 minutes or half an hour **somewhere**. It could be in-between folding the laundry and doing the dinner dishes, after the kids are (finally) in bed, taking a bubble bath and being alone with your thoughts.

Balance is about finding time in the daily grind to get as much done as you can, family time, couple time and self-time. Family time is about sharing, not necessarily expensive outings, but talking around the dinner table, playing games on a "family night", taking the dog for a walk together, reading bed-time stories together, cooking or baking together, doing family chores together as a "team", Sunday brunches made together or a relaxing "tea party" with your child to "catch up" on friends and school.

Couple time can be harder. It doesn't have to be a formal "date" with a babysitter, although that would be a nice idea every couple of weeks or monthly, something to look forward to. After the kids are in bed, a few "stolen moments" cuddling quietly or chatting about life, how you're feeling, in a bubble bath, in bed or in front of the fire goes a long way to staying connected. Remember, you may be parents, but you're also still a couple!

Self-time is anything you can fit in or schedule in that you enjoy, whether it's reading a magazine while the laundry is in the dryer, knitting while you're watching the kids' swimming lesson, or just sitting quietly with a pet on your lap while the soup is simmering. Weekends can be a challenge, with "catch-up" time for things left from the week to do. I am always impressed by parents who "spell each other off", one sleeping in on Saturday while the other gets the kids fed and occupied, and the other taking turns on the Sunday. What a wonderful caring way to give each other individual time!

Balance is also about "head and heart" for me, both within yourself and in your relationships. This means being capable of thinking emotionally (with your heart) and intellectually/rationally (with your head) and listening to both, balancing it out. Thinking in one mode without the other is incomplete and unbalanced, not accessing all that you **know** from within yourself. This principle also extends to relationships, when one partner is more "head-" or "heart-" dominant in thinking and it can lead to some major misunderstandings, assumptions and miscommunication. I often find that in working with couples, I became the universal translator, helping each to understand the other's point-of-view, whether it's the emotional side or the rational/intellectual side. Sometimes it's a totally different language that is hard for them to express and be understood. That's why figuring it out within yourself is so important to be able to put both sides together.

Balance internally, in your thoughts, your feelings, your activities, your time, your wants and needs is hard to achieve but crucial to your emotional, physical and mental health. It takes care and attention, self-respect, and self-nurturance but you're worth it! Balance externally, in our lives, our relationships, and our families also shows respect: for ourselves and others. It's hard to constantly maintain it, but getting back to that equilibrium that feels right and keeps you happy is what life is all about.

Chapter 17:

Putting It All Together: Fitting Together the Pieces of the Puzzle

Well, now I've shared many of the parts of what I know, what I feel, what I believe and what I've learned through the years. It's time to put the pieces together, like the pieces of the puzzle I help people put together about their lives. As I sit here with my daughter's kitten snuggled and purring contentedly on my lap, I can't help but marvel at how easy a pet's life is compared to ours. There is no mystery for them: they are happy just being fed and watered, given a clean place to sleep and toilet themselves, opportunities to play, and the chance to be loved and show us love. It's a simple balance: if we're good to them, they're good to us. No illusions, no assumptions, no miscommunication. Sometimes I think life would be great to come back as a beloved pet the second-time around.

Our lives are so much more complex. Now that's the understatement of the year! The first step to putting everything together is taking stock of your life, watching it flow past like a video movie of all of your memories. Fast-forwarding and rewinding as necessary, watch the story of your life unfold. There are reasons for our behaviors that stem from past experiences, repeating or changing old patterns. Understanding and recognizing where our lives began, where we came from, what our family was like, how we were raised, how we were as children, what our school experiences were like, who our friends were, what our teen years were like, our first loves and heartaches, our careers, our relationships, the births of our children all trace the flow of our lives. Could we have changed something, anything to make it better? What have we learned, what should we have learned, what have we become, who are we becoming? This is the puzzle of each of our lives.

Understanding what makes us who we are is just the beginning. Knowing who we are now, how we feel about our lives, what we want, what needs are still unmet, is the next step. Do you like who you are or have become? Do you enjoy your life? Do you survive in it, just existing or are you living it to its fullest? Do you know what you want in life that would make you happier? Are all of your needs met, and if not, do you know how to meet them? Are your relationships fulfilling, and if not, what would make them even better? Answering these questions honestly for yourself, once you have understood your past will help you work towards an even better future. Only you can make it happen because only you have lived your past and felt it all.

Counseling helps people to understand what it has taken to bring them into the present, to identify what has worked, and what hasn't. They come to understand how they feel about every aspect of their lives: about themselves, their relationships, their families, their careers, about their futures. They find out what they're searching for, what they want in their lives, what they need to feel happier, more fulfilled, more successful, to feel better about themselves. They identify what their "symptoms" mean, to understand and take control of them, not to be controlled by them. They learn that caring about themselves, for themselves is not selfish and that selflessness leads to self-denial and unhappiness.

People need to grow, to make changes in themselves and their lives for **themselves**. Being told to change feels like an ultimatum and can lead to resentment. It needs to happen at your own pace. If someone can't accept you for who you are, they have a decision to make: to wait for you to grow in your own time or love you for who you are, with all your flaws.

Our feelings are there to tell us something that should not be ignored. Emotional pain, sadness and anxiety are there for a reason and they have to be listened to, just like physical pain. If something hurts, something needs to change so these emotions don't rule your life. Habits can be good or bad are simply ways of relieving emotions like anxiety, sadness or pain. They can be changed so that they don't rule your life.

Please remember to listen to yourself **intently** and make sure it's you who you're hearing (your "inner voice"). Old "ghosts from the past", negative messages and judgments can revolve around in our heads and rule our lives, holding us back from who we are, who we're meant to be. Rewrite them and cheer yourself on!

All relationships take commitment to ensure that the "four cornerstones" of communication, honesty, respect, and trust are in balance. Nurture them, work on them together to keep on growing together, not apart. Relationships change and grow with the addition of children, just as we grow into becoming parents. Work together as a team to ensure that you continue to grow together as a couple at the same time. Listen to your children, to understand them and help them understand themselves. Remember that life is an ongoing growth process and that we don't stop learning, changing or growing until the day that we die.

If you're not happy, do something about it! Find your passion, what you want, what you need to feel more complete. Look inside yourself, not to others to complete you or make you feel better. No one knows you like you do, so be assertive about it! Balance your time, your relationships, your "head and heart" and don't ignore yourself. Find your own equilibrium that works for you.

This is where the beautiful Serenity Prayer comes in: having the courage to change what you can (the future), to accept what you can't (the past), and the wisdom to know the difference. The past can't be changed but how we deal with it can by learning to forgive if we can't forget. Blame and guilt just hold us back, trapping the energy in the past when we need it for the present and to motivate us for the future ahead. I wish you the courage, the energy and wisdom to find your own true self and happiness. Enjoy the journey along the way...

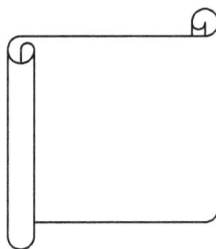

www.ingramcontent.com/pod-product-compliance
Lightning Source LLC
Chambersburg PA
CBHW060510030426
42337CB00015B/1837